some
where

First published in New Zealand in 2019 under the title *Somewhere: Women's Stories of Migration* by Beatnik Publishing (ISBN 9780995118034)

Canadian edition published in 2020 by Brindle & Glass, an imprint of TouchWood Editions

Brindle & Glass
An imprint of TouchWood Editions
touchwoodeditions.com

The information in this book is true and complete to the best of the authors' knowledge. All recommendations are made without guarantee on the part of the authors or the publisher.

Design and typesetting: Beatnik Design Ltd.
Creative director and illustrator: Sally Greer
Design updates: Sydney Barnes

CATALOGUING DATA AVAILABLE FROM LIBRARY AND ARCHIVES CANADA

ISBN 9781927366936 (print)
ISBN 9781927366943 (electronic)

TouchWood Editions acknowledges that the land on which we live and work is within the traditional territories of the Lkwungen (Esquimalt and Songhees), Malahat, Pacheedaht, Scia'new, T'Sou-ke and W̱SÁNEĆ (Pauquachin, Tsartlip, Tsawout, Tseycum) peoples.

We acknowledge the financial support of the Government of Canada through the Canada Book Fund and the Canada Council for the Arts, and of the Province of British Columbia through the British Columbia Arts Council and the Book Publishing Tax Credit.

The interior pages of this book have been printed on 100% post-consumer recycled paper, processed chlorine free, and printed with vegetable-based inks.

Printed in Canada

24 23 22 21 20   1 2 3 4 5

Somewhere

Stories of Migration by Women from Around the World

Edited by
Lorna Jane Harvey

&

BRINDLE
AND
GLASS

Contents

Foreword

Rt Hon.
Helen Clark

Migration is a major phenomenon of our times. More than 258 million people were estimated to be international migrants in 2017 —that was up from 173 million in 2000. While the percentage rise is less dramatic because of the world's rapid population growth, nonetheless the overall numbers are significant.

So often, migration is spoken of in pejorative terms, and denounced by populists for political reasons. Yet objective assessments of migration suggest that, in general, where it is regularized, it benefits both the source and the destination countries, and can be very positive for human development.

Many migrants, however, have not left their homes voluntarily. We live in times of unprecedented forced displacement—seventy million people are forcibly displaced by war, conflict, and/or repression and human rights abuses.

This is a crisis with global implications, and those impacted by it need international solidarity. We need to look beyond the numbers to the human face of this crisis. The provision of shelter, food, water, and sanitation is vital. As well, the forcibly displaced have many more needs which must be met to uphold human dignity.

Then, for those on the move in search of work and opportunity, not all are able to access regular and legal means of migration. As we regularly see on our television screens, there are many desperate and dangerous journeys to lands where the migrants then face a precarious existence and often outright discrimination and exploitation.

The collection of stories in the pages of this book gives voice to women migrants. Some of the stories speak of forced displacement, while others are about deliberate and voluntary migration. Those who have written have shown courage, resilience, and strength. May their stories inspire strength in the many others in similar situations around the world.

Rt Hon. Helen Clark
Former Prime Minister of New Zealand

Introduction

Lorna Jane Harvey

Migration touches people at their very core. It tears an individual from everything they know; it resets expectations, forces them to adapt to a new way of life. The value of traditions and cultural and social norms changes. It's a massive adaptation for any individual to migrate. Whether the migration is from one country to a similar one or between very different cultures, there will be significant adjustment.

From the refugee to the economic migrant, I have encountered so many migrants of so many different backgrounds and circumstances. Migration is one of the defining global issues of the early twenty-first century, as, according to the International Organization for Migration, more people are migrating now than at any other point in human history. In recent years, Northern African and Middle Eastern conflicts and tensions have led to millions of refugees relocating. A generation ago, Europe was inundated by migrants from the Balkans as former Yugoslavia was broken by civil war.

I have immigrated three times, and I'm a citizen of as many countries. I became a migrant for probably the same reason as nearly every other migrant: to improve my life in some way. For some, the relocation is a desperate attempt at survival, as when refugees flee from war-torn regions or political or racial discrimination. For many others, relocation is planned because they believe a better, fuller or richer experience awaits in the new land. Most long for improvement of some kind, however difficult the transition may be.

Since beginning to compile this anthology and writing my contributing essay, I have left Switzerland and migrated to New Zealand. It has been a complete reset for me. What is appropriate, social norms and so much more have to be reassimilated. In Switzerland, I was an elected councillor. I knew what the polite way to enter a meeting was, how to run events, whether it was necessary to stay for drinks after meetings. I knew which formality to employ when meeting new people, whether to shake their hand or give them three kisses depending on context and relationship, which kinds of foods to cook when inviting friends for a meal. I knew how the culture, tradition and society worked. Since I've also lived in Canada for nearly two decades, I feel as comfortable and able to navigate society there as I do in Switzerland. Although I recognize that New Zealand is more similar to Canada and Switzerland than India or Russia, for example, this last move has reminded me just how unsettling migration is. I spend a significant amount of my time trying to understand my new environment and helping my family feel at home in their new country. I chose to migrate to New Zealand and feel immensely grateful for being here, but I can't pretend it didn't rattle, stress and try me. I will figure out how my new surroundings function a little more each day, and in time I will make true friendships once again. I will rebuild a whānau (family), as they say here, but I can't pretend it isn't tough, even though my migrations have all happened in fairly positive circumstances compared to many others'.

I was inspired to compile this anthology because I believe the implications of migration, especially for women, are often unknown, unheard, unspoken. Many women are mere shadows when they migrate, and their personal experiences remain silent. I thought writing from my own experience alone would be incomplete. Watching the stories come together as I compiled this anthology confirmed this.

This book doesn't pretend to cover every type of migration. It's a small window into the world of women's migrations, a topic that is rarely addressed. There are treasures of wisdom to be gleaned from their experiences, and there is heartfelt honesty within their stories. Perhaps their words will give you hope, encourage or inspire you, or simply give you insight into a globally relevant and important subject on a personal level, rather than through distant, abstract news stories.

The women who contributed to this anthology come from varied backgrounds, and their immigrations have stemmed from many things, such as adventure, economic gains or fleeing for their safety. Their homes include New Zealand, Australia, the UK, Canada, the USA, Switzerland, Ukraine, Hong Kong, Japan, Syria and many more places. Some are single mothers, some are at the heart of wealthy families, and some were children when they were forced to uproot. There are some recurrent patterns through all the stories—retaining inherited identities while adapting to new cultures, new people, new lands. There are also some important divergences, as some migrants feel an intense need to belong and assimilate, while others don't seem to perceive any alienation at all. The migrant sometimes feels like a stranger to herself as she recreates herself and her home, and clings to other aspects of her former life. All have one thing in common: they are strong women who have made a new life because of their migration. The relocation has brought joy, stress and a sense of gain and loss to most of them.

Some of the writers are friends, others I approached for this anthology because I admired their work and their strength, and some were recommended through connections. I have grown to respect and admire every one of them, and I feel privileged to know them. They are all amazing, and I believe you will be touched by their stories.

Lorna Jane Harvey

Dr. Rita Sebestyén

The Jewellery Box

Ready to Run

There is a jewellery box on my impeccable white chest of drawers, in Helsingør, Denmark, where I currently live. It contains a set of large, tightly strung, perfectly oval burnished beads of mountain crystals and another string of huge, natural, rustic fluorite stones, alternated with small silver gems. There's a long coral necklace and an even longer genuine pearl one. There are some Murano medals, more genuine pearl jewellery and loads of amber in different colours and from different origins. These are my favourites to look at in this minimalist three-storey acacia casket. The box is also filled with earrings, bracelets and brooches. I haven't worn them for three years now.

My ten-year-old daughter often sneaks in shyly and asks if she and her friends can play with them. They can. She always reassures me that they will not touch the flamboyant hundred-year-old hand-crafted neo-baroque ring with the huge ruby stone. The one that is passed from generation to generation between the women in my family. We receive it—and the right to wear it—when we turn thirty. The ruby ring is the only asset of my once wealthy and noble family that has not been destroyed by war, taken away by communization or lost on gambling or while in refuge. The metaphor of us, being strong and repressing and proud. Survival. Exclamation mark. Signpost.

My homeland is Romania. Beyond its financial value, jewellery has always been the succinct bearer of identity for many of us Armenians, Turks, Romani people, Jews, Greeks, Germans and

Hungarians. It shows taste, roots, social class, nationality. In times when we have to run, we put on all our jewellery and fasten our kids to our bodies. And then we run.

My Grandmother
From the Top of the Wardrobe
1943. Arad, Romania, is occupied by the Nazis. My grandfather's surname is Steindl. The family is proud of being descendants of the famous German architect Steindl, who designed the Hungarian parliament, also in a very flamboyant neo-baroque style. His ancestors were brought to Romania by Maria Theresia to build solid, strong, good-looking edifices in the country. No one is more obviously German than my grandfather. He is a good Catholic. He almost started seminary to become a Catholic priest, but he met my grandmother. Her mother died long ago, and her father disappeared soon after in the Brazilian jungle, chasing a mysterious blonde woman. My well-respected, good Catholic grandfather marries this orphan. She's a stubborn young woman with a wavy bob and long, slender, suntanned neck. By 1943, they have a six-year-old son. As the Nazi threat gets closer, my grandfather takes part in a series of baptisms-in-bulk, becoming the godfather of around forty Jewish friends of his. But name matters, and my grandfather is very much wanted by the Nazis to join their forces in Arad. He immediately leaves for Budapest, Hungary. He is recorded as a deserter.

Little by little, so as not to get noticed and become suspicious to the authorities, my grandmother sells the furniture and everything she inherited and gathered, except for the ruby ring. She gives all her money to smugglers, fastens her six-year-old son to her body, puts on the ruby ring and heads to the border. A couple of hundred metres away from the border, the smuggler leaves the small group of deserters, Jews and resistants to their own devices, taking all their money. They split up in smaller groups to enhance their chances of crossing the border unseen. My grandmother's son whines, so they give him some shots of pálinka (strong distilled alcohol) to shut him up. He starts coughing and crying. The group is frightened by the noise-making boy who threatens to give them away. They evaporate instantly. My grandmother starts marching through the fields, in a random direction, with her son fastened on to her body and the ruby ring on her finger. She manages to cross the border and is taken on to a chariot by peasants. They reach the first village, where she is immediately turned in to the authorities. She is warned in time by some villagers, so, without hesitation, without a rest, she escapes and continues her journey. She changes trains at every station and, after a couple of weeks, reaches Budapest (220 kilometres from Arad). She finds my grandfather, who works there, undercover, as a tailor in a classy saloon.

My mother is conceived, and Budapest is taken under siege. When not in the basement, waiting for the aerial attacks to cease, at least for a while, my grandmother climbs up on the highest wardrobe in their rented apartment and jumps down, trying to abort my mother. She is unsuccessful, and my mother is born in Budapest, under the siege, in 1944.

After the war is over, the family of now four members returns to Arad. The journey takes a couple of weeks again. They have no money left. The transport systems have not really been restored yet, so they take different freight trains, hide in the wagons. During the long stops in the fields, my grandfather gets off the wagon and picks vegetables he finds, and my grandmother cooks soup on a fire set between the train lines. By the time they reach Arad, my mother has club feet and a huge belly and head, and is extremely underweight. The family spends any money they can scrape together to get her a doctor. He finds that my mother has rickets. The prognosis is not good: she will die soon.

My Mother

The Smell of the Washing Powder

1960s. In Arad, my mother has become a biology teacher. She was cured of rickets, she married my father at the age of seventeen, and together they attended the most prestigious university in Romania, pursuing a correspondence education, as they had to work all the time. She sings Communist songs, her favourite being "The Chariots are Carrying the Hay," but soon gets very critical of the political system. My parents end up as teachers in a small village next to the Hungarian-Romanian border.

Before the revolution in 1989, my mother witnesses the torture of the Romanians who try to pass the border illegally and get caught by the Romanian guards in the peak of the Ceauşescu dictatorship. Her nephew—the son of the six-year-old boy from the first story—comes to our house one summer evening in 1987. He asks us to lend him the fantastic binoculars we managed to smuggle across the border a year earlier (as binoculars and, for example, typewriters are not allowed to be kept in households in Romania). There is a long, closed family discussion. My parents suspect what the binoculars are for. They decide not to lend them to him. The next morning, a group of unsuccessful illegal border-crossers are caught again. They have to march, while chained together by their ankles, and sing Communist songs. My mother does not dare to look in their direction. We stay glued to the Hungarian radio, which broadcasts a series of interviews with the ones who managed to cross the border. My mother recognizes her nephew's voice.

After the turn in 1989, my mother continues teaching biology. She was raised a materialist, a Darwinist, throughout her whole education. My grandfather's Catholicism had vanished a long time ago, seen by my family as a fairy-tale worldview. The turn brings religion, both traditional and new, back into the society. Worldviews clash on all platforms and in the schools, too. My mother is bewildered and conflicted. She refuses to fight; instead, she invites a priest to her classes so they can present together. I think she hopes for spirituality.

She had been on the verge of giving up teaching, but soon she is given hours in the high school she also attended, and, because of her struggles and honesty, she becomes a respected member of the community.

Post-socialist Romania does not live up to the great expectations of a tortured and oppressed society's dreams. In the early nineties, my father wants to leave for Hungary, where both he and my mother would get better pay and more respected positions before retirement. But I want to stay; I have just been admitted to the same well-known Romanian university they attended. We all stay. A couple of years later, my parents retire and are on the verge of starvation. My grandmother, from the first story, ends up living with them. She has been a widow for twenty years now, and she also buried her son, the one she carried on her body across the border. I receive a scholarship in Hungary, so I move there and soon get married. Meanwhile, my parents start their first vacation after their retirement. They have planned it and saved for it for years. They leave, and the next day, my grandmother, who is being nursed by the neighbour, walks out of her room and into the kitchen, something she has not done for at least three years. She sings a couple of her favourite childhood songs, walks back into her room, leans back on the sofa and dies.

Hungary joins the EU, but Romania does not yet. My parents are devastated by the thought that we are now separated by a newly established Iron Curtain. They want to sell their apartment and move to Hungary. There is a considerable gap between the living standards of the two countries, and they will hardly manage to buy a decent home with the money they have gathered all their lives. Still, they sell their apartment, their furniture and everything movable. The amount of money they get is pathetic.

They put all they have left into their old Citroën. There is a huge queue at the border, and they are exhausted. The border guard checks them out and lets them cross the border through the fields, only a couple of kilometres away from the place my grandma crossed illegally more than half a century ago.

It is Christmas in Budapest, Hungary, 2003. My mother and my father are sleeping on the inflatable bed in the dining room in the home I share with my husband. They have bought a house next to the Hungarian-Romanian border, but it is not yet in a state to live in. I have to be the landlady now, so I eagerly keep carrying huge packages and bags from all the shops to cater for all. We do not talk too much. My mother gives me the ruby ring and an old art deco intarsia box. I search the box carefully and I find a picture of my grandmother there: an orphan, a stubborn young woman with a wavy bob and long, slender, suntanned neck.

My mother is awake all night. In the morning, she says she could not sleep because of the smell of the washing powder I bought in bulk to wash all the clothes and things for their new life.

Me

Time to Sell the Flat

At the end of the nineties, at twenty-six, after finishing university, I became a lecturer and well-known dramaturge and artist in Romania. Still, in 1998, I left for Hungary with a very small PhD scholarship. At thirty, I married a Hungarian man who became a manager at a Western European company. My grandma died, and my parents moved to Hungary and made a nice new home for themselves, with a huge garden where my mother could experiment and practice her skills in biology, specializing in botany. There was a year when she, by mistake, produced almost a hundred kilograms of green peas.

Safety is the most important thing, we keep telling each other, and I try to believe it.

Safety is a complex notion for us: It means that we are part of the world where there is no dictatorship, war or abuse; it also means that the core family stays in the same country, not separated by impenetrable geographical or political borders. It means that we can freely speak our mother tongue and not be discriminated against, that we can trust the laws will protect us, too, and that we can pursue our professions and provide for ourselves and our children. It means that we can walk down the street without fear, people will nod at us as part of the community, we can sit down in a café and be served exactly like anyone else, and we can keep our promise to buy a cake for a child.

I am convinced that I can have it all in Budapest, that it is enough to work hard. But my career gets stuck; I cannot proceed in the Hungarian society at all. I get more and more frustrated and angry and closed into my own world. My life is torn into two pieces: There is an appearance of a successful woman, and there is the constant, inherent restlessness of losing perspective. I teach English and coach in communication, only in our home, which is now an upper-middle-class, art deco-style designer flat in the heart of Budapest, in the new Jewish district. In the end, I work at the National Theatre, start a theatrical journal and get a book published on the early adolescence of my grandmother from the first story, but I never feel at ease, or at home.

In 2007, I give birth to our only daughter, which isolates me even more. By the time she is six, it's obvious that the Hungarian government will proceed in their right-wing, nationalistic politics, and I want my daughter to be raised in a free world, so I persuade my husband to move to Denmark, to the headquarters of his company. We follow him after eight months.

In the summer of 2013, I get off the plane with my daughter. I smell the salty air and the moistness of the sea and observe the clearness of the sky. I am convinced that geographical settings have to do with states of mind, and I make up my mind to finally pursue my own life. After three years of struggle, depression, panic and torture, we are now getting divorced and, as a first step, I move into the small, white, minimalist room downstairs in my husband's rented apartment, along with the jewellery box. As my grandmother's art deco jewellery box had fallen apart, I bought this minimalist acacia one, and I placed the ruby ring into it. I am working towards getting all the papers, work, the residence permit and my daughter's school arranged, as well as selling the art deco flat in Budapest. Within six months, I will be moving into my own rental in Helsingor, together with our daughter.

My Daughter

Not Julia

I am deeply frightened by recognizing the patterns in my family, especially those that affect the women—oppression, rape, harassment, not able to work to provide for ourselves. The ruby ring follows us all as we pass it on. I do not know its actual financial worth, and, after some hesitation, I decided not to ever take it to the jeweller to be estimated. It could be worth something between half a year's wage in Romania and ten times more: half a year's wage in Denmark. My mother warned me that the ring came with the maturity of never selling it or exchanging it, whatever came. The ring is us. The patterns are us. They follow us all as a vicious heritage. Even when reading articles for my theatrical work, I stumble into research papers stating that, according to neuroscientific discoveries, we pass the trauma on through our genes, too. No matter what we decide rationally, the shocks will change our cells and genes to haunt us throughout generations.

We also had, as women coming from a noble, famous and proud family, a middle name: Julia. Since all women in Eastern Europe used to lose their surnames and take on their husband's names when they married, our proud, famous and noble family used this middle name for the women, to mark them, to pass it on, to make sure that they represented the bloodline. My daughter has only one first name, a name that sounds almost funny in Hungarian—lots of people laughed at us when they first heard it—but one that is used and well known in many other countries and languages. No middle name at all. I am contemplating what to do with the ruby ring.

Diana Ruiz

Broken Cycles

The students' hearts raced as they waited for the signal from their professor, Thay. "Now!" she shouted at noon, and they all threw their desks and chairs out of the window, two floors down, on to the street below. Thay wasn't scared. Castro's men would have to take them all, the teacher and students, if they came.

At first Thay and her family were happy with Castro's revolution and his ideas, but she soon realized it wasn't right. The Chinese saw it first—they felt Castro's ideology had flipped. Her family was close to many Chinese-Cubans. There was a large Chinese population in Cuba that immigrated for contract work to replace or sometimes work alongside African slaves. When slavery was abolished in 1886, they met the demand for labour. Thay didn't believe them at first, but it became evident they had been right. Castro's revolution soon yielded a Communist Cuba where anyone who disagreed was punished, probably executed. The anti-revolution demonstrations were coordinated but short-lived.

Fernando, Thay's fiancé, was an engineering student who fought against Castro's regime, along with Thay's brothers. He was a political activist, blew up bridges and eventually was part of a group of twenty men who hijacked a plane to Mexico. Che Guevara executed Thay's father when he couldn't find Fernando and Thay's brothers, who were in hiding, heading towards Miami.

Thay taught architecture at Havana University. She was well educated, beautiful and the most intelligent one of the family. She observed things quietly, didn't believe in gossip or shunning. She perceived people differently from most, knew when they didn't believe what they were saying, refused to give attention to falseness. She was fascinated by physics and thought beyond the possibilities of the possibilities. She was, in her own quiet way, involved in the movement against Castro. That day when she asked her students to throw their furniture out of the window was probably her most outspoken fight. She was unlike many who protested loudly in the streets: She fought in her own discreet way. She wrote and printed propaganda against Castro's regime, and when Castro's men came to the house, she hid the printing machine, moving it from one room to another as they searched.

The situation deteriorated, and Thay and her family feared for their safety. They managed to get passage to Colombia, where a distant family member welcomed them for a time. Thay, along with her mother and sisters, stayed in Colombia at first. But Thay's love waited for her in Miami, and Thay eventually joined him.

She was sponsored and helped by some religious organizations. When they saw what a good cook Thay was, they encouraged her to enter a pie-baking competition, which she won. When they asked what the magic ingredient was, she said, "Rum, of course!"

Thay and Fernando married in Miami. So many were migrating to Florida at that time that it was incredibly poor. People were near starvation. They gathered on Sundays with family and scraped together all their resources for a meal so they could eat meat once a week. It might only be goat or fish, but they tried to celebrate their new life despite the disabling poverty. Thay and Fernando knew Miami was too precarious, so they moved to Los Angeles and started a new life together.

They had three children, and by the time I was five years old, they had separated. I was the eldest. Fernando was what Cubans would have called a pretty boy, a man from the middle or upper class with many mistresses. Thay refused to be part of such a marriage. She was the first woman in her family to plant a stake and say no. She would not live like that. Her father had been a tyrant, and now her husband wanted to treat her disrespectfully. She refused. She wanted a better life for herself and her children. Fernando, who eventually became a clinical psychologist, earned a good living. He had warned and threatened Thay when she filed for divorce, telling her if she left, he wouldn't support the family. She stated that she would go hungry before living a life absent of integrity.

All the women of the family who came to America had similar trouble with their husbands, but they chose different ways to deal with the situation. One aunt laced her husband's espresso with sleeping pills so he'd be too sleepy to go out with his mistress. Another slipped Valium into her husband's food to quell his violent temper. One aunt gave her husband laxatives to interrupt his drinking sprees and once even rolled him up in a quilt when he passed out and beat him with a rolling pin (no bruises). Each of the women had their own way of surviving and exercising control.

Thay taught piano and sold consignment jewellery, but soon finances slipped and we were forced to give up our large house and move to a run-down one-bedroom house. She also had to give up her rented piano. She was devastated, but she kept fighting quietly for a decent life. She slept on the couch, making sure her children had their own bedroom. She took a few college classes when time permitted. Thay opened her home to people from all religions and walks of life. She believed different was good. I think people were her form of entertainment. She loved cooking while listening to her guests. She'd never criticize. She observed, sometimes smiling to herself. But if people gossiped or acted inappropriately, she quickly removed herself from the situation.

My brother Herman was hit by a car and spent several months in a coma. Part of his skull had to be replaced. Our small family took turns by his bedside so he'd never be alone. We basically lived in the hospital.

Thay spent eighteen years attending university in the end. She studied physics and was offered a position at Las Vegas University. We moved to Nevada and settled into a new, if isolated, life. We were now miles from our friends and the few family members who had joined us in Los Angeles.

While it seemed that a better chapter in our life was unfolding, things quickly began to crumble. Thay began to speak of being watched, of cameras in the television and throughout the house. She saw cars follow her as she walked home from work. I was twelve years old, and I believed my mother. I showered in the dark, dressed in my closet, believed cars followed me from school. Her symptoms became my reality.

Years of survival, great sacrifices, fear, migration, stress and sorrow had taken their toll on Thay. She was diagnosed with paranoid schizophrenia and institutionalized. I was dispatched to my dad's, and my brothers to different aunts. The family broke. My brothers and I fought to return home to live with our mother once she was released. Once back home, I quickly realized that she was not the same. She was heavily sedated and slept a lot. When we were children, our mother had been very involved with us, playing games and even participating in our play dress-up. She did eventually adjust to the medicine and become more herself, but that took a few years. We were forced to move into the projects, government-funded housing with hundreds of people in precarious social or financial situations. The area looked clean, as it was new, but soon after we saw crime rates increase and it became unsafe. I was thirteen and left much to my own devices as my mom struggled with mental illness.

I found new friends in the projects, friends I would never normally have been allowed to hang out with, but since Thay wasn't really present, no one told me off. The first time I had sexual relations, I had no idea what had happened. I had absolutely no knowledge of how things worked, of my body. I soon got pregnant. The father of the child was almost eighteen. He should have gone to jail, but instead the judge decreed that we were to be married in a Mormon church. I was thirteen, and it was illegal to marry at that age, yet the Mormons used their political influence to make it happen, and I went along with it all. In a way, I felt happy that I was going to have a baby, since I had no one else after my family structure had fallen apart. I had a son, lived in an apartment in the projects and realized that my husband was crazy and did drugs but didn't really know what that meant. When Thay's mental state was good, she helped me a little, taught me how to be a parent. One day, I called my mother in a panic because the whites of my three-month-old's eyes had turned orange. I had fed him a whole jar of baby food well before the age where he should have been eating solids.

After a year, things were getting too crazy, with drugs and more, so I left my husband and moved back in with my mother.

I entered a secretarial program and was offered public housing. I lived in the same area as my mother. A year later, my mom was offered a new opportunity in Miami, and she asked me to come as well. I couldn't leave because my ex-husband had managed to get legal custody of our son, even though our son was living with me and only went to his father's on weekends. The environment was unsafe: drugs and little parenting. A friend in Las Vegas with connections got my son and me false identification, and we fled, first to Colorado and then on to Florida to join my mother and brothers. Thay was doing well; she was lucid. She was managing the household, until one of my brothers (the one who'd been hit by a car a few years earlier) developed severe neck ache. As the pain progressed, my mother became convinced that it was linked to the car-accident injuries. She decided he needed to see the specialist who had operated on him after the car crash and moved back to Los Angeles.

I needed to return to Los Angeles too to be with my family. I contacted a lawyer, who sorted out my divorce and was able to get me full custody of my son so we could return using our real identification. My brother Herman had been diagnosed with a malignant tumour and later died of cancer. A year later, my youngest brother, Ian, was hit by a car and died as well. In a two-year period, both brothers were gone.

Thay held it together for a year. She was in university full-time. Then, all of a sudden, she broke. From that point on, there was no going back. She was in and out of mental institutions for the rest of her life. At the end of her life, she was paralyzed after suffering several strokes. She died at sixty-five.

I had a second child when I was nineteen. A daughter. That was when I finally stopped lying about my age, as well. No one would have hired me if I had told them I was fourteen, sixteen, eighteen.

Until I was about twenty-five, I did little more than survive. Then, there came a time when I felt stable in my life. I'd had a difficult childhood, and as a young adult, I had witnessed so many horrible things taking place: A friend was murdered, another raped, a few were taken into sexual trafficking, others were affected by drug addiction, AIDS took a cousin and suicides were common. As a result of seeing so much domestic violence, neglect, teenage pregnancies, mental health issues and abuse, I became an advocate. I fought against injustice. At first, people came to me from within my family, then from the wider community, to speak on their behalf. I helped establish campaigns for representation in areas that affected women and children. Later, when my children were adults, I studied organizational behaviour and development. I know now that these experiences inform my role as CEO and founder of WGLI (Women's Global Leadership Initiative). To this day, if someone is in trouble, I make time to help out, and there's always a place to stay in my home. Building self-confidence in others is one of my greatest objectives in life.

It was important to acknowledge my history, but it was just as important to break the destructive patterns that had led my mother and me to so many painful places. I decided there would be no more secrets in my family.

In 2006, a year after my mother passed, I went on a journey to Spain and Italy with my father, who had been diagnosed with amyotrophic lateral sclerosis (ALS). As the trip progressed, the disease took hold and became more debilitating. We spent the last days in Rome before returning home. Each morning, while at breakfast in the hotel in Rome, I watched a group of men argue. I was drawn by their passionate debate and the power of the foreign language they spoke. I finally approached them, and they told me they were from the Balkan region and were discussing politics. I told them I'd studied their culture: the Byzantine, the Ottoman Empire, the wars that predictably happened every seventy-five years. I had even interviewed women who had been systematically raped to annihilate a race. Their stories stayed with me. I'd often say, "I will go there one day," feeling an overwhelming sorrow. The men mocked me as only an intellectual, telling me that all of this knowledge was useless unless I went to the region to see for myself. I told them I wasn't ready. But everything I'd been through and everything I'd learned was in preparation for going there. They were right, and I knew it, and so, after my father passed, I went. When I first walked about Split, it felt as if the ground were vibrating - as if something were about to give, come apart. It was an intensity I had not felt before. While at the sea, I also experienced a sense of being at the earth's core. As the waves hit the shore and in turn receded, mirroring my inhalation and exhalation, I realized this was some form of higher consciousness, a spiritual experience. A calm and lightness I had never known.

My life was changed forever. I went home to America, but I knew I had to be in Croatia. I was ready, and so I moved there shortly afterwards.

I lived in Croatia on and off for four years and created a community of responsible women from all societal classes, who were encouraged to come together and realize that, at the end of the day, they were all from the same village. They were united by similar concerns and experiences, and by a desire for change for their community, their futures and their children.

As I worked there, an elderly retired professor who often spoke with me said, "I know why you're working here. It's so that one day you can work in Cuba. One day, Cuba will be post-socialism. People will not know how to defend themselves or how to do anything for themselves. They won't have any context or knowledge of how organizational systems could help society. They'll want to feed their families, and they won't be able to rely on the government like they have, like we had."

And I realized then that she was right. About seven years ago, after working all over the Balkan region, I finally went to Cuba. The beginning of the end of the system was taking place. In the homes, all the conversations seemed to be about exiting the country. They'd tell tourists that everything was fine, but that just wasn't the reality.

It is my dream to one day empower women in Cuba. I'm connected to women entrepreneurs to help establish an organized collective to share resources, and, as the country changes, they'll be better prepared. It will take at least a generation for the country to break free from post-socialism survival and learn new, healthier ways to function. I don't live there—my home is in San Francisco—but I want to continue helping women globally and especially in Cuba.

Migration can enrich lives just as it can shatter them. New lives, old pains and new challenges emerge. Education can mean nothing or everything. Standards of living are usually thrown to the wind. For a time, anyway. For a month, a few years, a generation or two. But old and new cultures always seem to remain strong.

We islanders, my parents and my children included, believe that we belong everywhere. We would all be willing to die for the principle of freedom. My children see themselves as Cuban-Americans. We have the ability to connect and talk to anyone, from a president to a farm worker. My mother showed us that communication, learning, discovering and accepting other people are of the utmost importance. If my parents suffered discrimination when they migrated, it was never spoken about. Through my parents' and my migrations, there doesn't seem to have been a conscious attempt to assimilate. We are unique, and we are content to belong to many cultures.

Kathinka Fossum Evertsen

Challenging Perceptions

The first thing you notice when you fly in over Bangladesh's capital, Dhaka, is water. Especially in the month of June. When you put your feet on the ground, it smells wet, like mud.

Living in the world's largest river delta, Bangladeshis know water. However, they have a limit as to how much water they can cope with. Bangladesh is ranked as one of the world's most vulnerable countries to climate change, and the southern part of the country is known to be especially vulnerable. The Bhola district, located about 225 kilometres south of Dhaka, is no exception. Situated where freshwater from the rivers meets saltwater from the Bay of Bengal, the district is exposed both to the activity of two rivers and to tidal changes and cyclones from the ocean.

During the summer of 2014, I spent time within the Bhola community, which is split between Bhola and migrant communities in larger cities in Bangladesh. I spoke to women who left their homes—and sometimes their families—in Bhola to take up wage work in Dhaka. They left when environmental degradation destroyed their land and houses. Here are some of their stories.

On Stilts

Bhola is naturally defined by Bhola Island. As Bhola is among the least developed districts in the country, there are only two ways to reach the island: by helicopter or by boat. Arriving early in the morning with the overnight ferry from Dhaka, we were hit by the morning fog. We tried to navigate among busy families and taxi drivers eager to give us a ride. Packing ourselves and our belongings into a tuk-tuk, we started driving from the very tip of the island along its eastern coast. The riverbank erosion was immediately visible. The river was eating its way into the asphalted road where we were driving. The embankment was filled with sacks of sand, now pouring out on to the beach along the riverbank. We were told that this embankment was built only five years ago.

We visited a small tea shop on stilts, on the side of the road. It had been rebuilt three times, we were told. "Why," I asked naïvely, "are you not rebuilding somewhere else? Say, on the other side of the embankment?" "This is the land I own," explained the owner. "I cannot move anywhere else. I have to stay here until I cannot rebuild anymore." I could only nod in response.

Changing weather challenges the way of life in Bhola. The main occupations are fishing and farming. The fisher communities make up the poorest population group in Bhola and they live close to the river, where land is cheap. Land along the riverbank is cheap because it is often lost to continual bank erosion. For the fishermen and their families, it also makes little sense to live far from the river, as fishing is the only livelihood available for poor families unable to buy farmland. According to villagers, to buy land a couple of kilometres inland is about five times more expensive than buying land in immediate proximity to the river.

According to the villagers, erosion has been increasing in recent years. The Meghna River strips soil from the island's eastern bank and, in the process, destroys farmland and displaces families. When asked where they grew up, people will often point into the river. Their childhood homes do not exist anymore, and many villagers explain how the river has forced them to move multiple times in their lives. The riverbank erosion is visible along the western coast of the island;

the river has eaten its way through farmland as well as asphalt like a bulldozer. When house and livelihood are rushed into the river, it may take a family decades to rebuild what was lost.

For some families, rebuilding becomes impossible. Those who have the means move farther inland. Many migrate longer distances, to cities like Khulna, Chittagong or Dhaka. Many go to the Bhola Slum in Dhaka, which is largely inhabited by people from the same northern part of Bhola, Ilisha. When a household has lost everything, it often happens that the whole household will move to an urban area. However, most households wish to stay. When the river is starting to cut close, one or a few household members often go to urban areas in order to earn and save up money for a new plot of land in preparation for the day the family will have to move.

Perceptions

Research shows that women are more vulnerable to negative consequences of climate change than men. Women who stay behind when the men move for work are often left with little resources and are vulnerable to harassment. The image of women as vulnerable make us think that women are unable to influence migration decisions, and it is often assumed men migrate while women stay behind when weather hits. This leads us to see women as passive, migrating only for the purpose of marriage or to accompany their husband, who migrates for work.

I was myself coloured by the mainstream perception of female migrants. First, I believed that few women migrated and that they did so only in exceptional cases. Next, I believed that female migrants would have in some way been sent by their families, as traditional gender norms in Bangladesh require male approval for women to leave the home. It turned out, however, that I was wrong on both counts. Numerous women migrate from the Bhola district to the Bhola Slum in Dhaka. Speaking to these women and their families, I discovered that female migrants had themselves taken the initiative to migrate and often had an important say in decision-making concerning both their own and their household's migration choices.

Life in Dhaka

During the beginning of my stay in Bangladesh, I was told that in a slum in the capital, Dhaka, women were moving on their own to take up wage work in the garment factories, leaving their villages in the southern Bhola district. I went to the Bhola Slum to see if I could find and talk to these women.

There are about five thousand different slums in Dhaka city. Mirpur, located on the western outskirts of the city, houses 405 of them, including the Bhola Slum. This slum was established during the 1980s and '90s, after the Bhola cyclone hit Bhola Island in 1971, displacing thousands of people from the district.

I spent about a month visiting the Bhola Slum on a nearly daily basis. There are only two entries to the slum, both fronting the main road. The road creates a natural border on one side of the slum, and a water channel does the same on the other side. Fenced by the road and the channel, the slum does not have much scope for expansion and is now more than full, housing about three thousand people. To create more space, people are constructing an extra floor on top of their tin sheds. According to World Vision, one of several NGOs working in the slum, this makes the Bhola Slum more dense and crowded than others in Dhaka. One aid worker explained to me how he resented going to the Bhola Slum because of its density. "The air is not moving!" he said. The roads within the slum are very narrow, muddy and filled with garbage.

Slum-dwellers face challenges conducting the routines of daily life, as they lack a stable supply of both water and electricity. During the time I visited the slum, the government had dug up the pipe from which the slum received its water. As the slum is an informal settlement, it does not receive water or electricity through formal channels, and it was not provided with an alternative supply when the government shut off the water. This meant slum-dwellers had to walk several kilometres to a nearby pond to bathe, until they found another pipe to drain clean water from.

The labour market in the Mirpur area has changed over time. When the Bhola Slum was first established, the area was under construction. This meant that men were in high demand in construction work. Now, the demand for construction workers in this area is low, leaving many male slum-dwellers without jobs.

Mirpur is also an area where numerous garment factories have been located. According to the slum-dwellers, garment factories prefer to employ women over men, so women have more stable-income opportunities than men in this area of Dhaka, in striking disagreement with gender norms in the rest of Bangladesh. Job prospects in Mirpur create a pull factor for women in the Bhola district, who see garment work as an alternative income opportunity when riverbank erosion threatens their families' livelihood. But, because of stricter labour regulations, factories are now shutting down or upgrading to other parts of the city, causing many slum-dwellers to lose their jobs.

Women's Stories

During one of my first days in the Bhola Slum, I spoke to a nineteen-year-old garment worker who had lived there for about a year. I will call her Sara. She explained how she and her older brother moved to Dhaka "because the river came close and we knew we would have to buy land." Her father had passed away about a year before, leaving the family without income earners. She had four younger siblings and her mother living in the village. Sara sent them half her salary every month. I asked her how she had decided that she would go to Dhaka. "First, I decided on my own. I have an uncle here. Back then, my father was still alive. I said I would go and come back alone, but my father and mother said no. My father said, 'No, we've raised you this far. We're going [to] arrange your marriage.' I said, 'No, I don't want to get married, I want to work.'" Sara smiled recalling how she had refused to do as her parents told her. "They said, 'You don't need to work.' Then I cried and told my grandmother and my older brother. Even my older brother wouldn't let me work. Then I said I would [go] myself. They asked me how I would get to Dhaka. I had a mobile phone and told them I would sell it and get money." She did just that, and when a neighbour girl told her she was going to Dhaka with her aunt, Sara went with them. "I told [my parents and brother], 'I have younger sisters, brothers; they have to be educated. We have to leave Bhola, so that's why I'll go.' I didn't listen to them." Sara smiled again. "I was happy that I left my village and came to Dhaka city. I liked it."

Another young garment worker, Tana, described a similar situation. Like Sara, she had lived in the slum for about a year. Tana had to migrate when her father passed away, since the family lost an important income with his death:

"I have a younger brother and sister . . . I had come to Dhaka city, so I can keep a good family, keep my brother and sister in school. There's a lot of sorrow in my family. I have lifted the anchor by coming to Dhaka and working. . . . I'll work so I can stand with my head held high. I can't give a lot, but the little bit I can do, I will. I'll only work for a few more years. I have my own future, you know? There is no father in that future to tell me. My mother can't do much. The little I can earn, I'm going to collect that."

There are no official numbers on internal migration in Bangladesh, and even less information about female migration in the country. During my three-and-a-half months conducting fieldwork there, I found indications that a substantial number of women migrated from Bhola. All respondents I spoke to knew someone who had migrated. A local government official in Bhola even suggested more women than men migrate. This includes young women like Tana and Sara, who migrate before marriage, but also women who migrate with their husbands. A less obvious aspect is that married women also influence decisions to migrate. I was told several stories where the women had been the initiative-takers in the household's decision to move to Dhaka. As Rushda, a thirty-five-year-old mother of four said matter-of-factly, "My husband working alone can't do it." She convinced her husband that the family needed to move to Dhaka, where they could both earn a wage. Others turned a deaf ear to their husbands' protests. Ayala explained: "If I listen to everything he says, I won't be able to raise my children."

Gender Trouble

The stories told by women who have migrated from Bhola show that the image of women as vulnerable may have blinded us from seeing that women can play a role in decision-making and that women, as well as men, are environmental migrants. However, although women and men alike migrate when their families' livelihoods are threatened, women are more vulnerable than men, both to the consequences of environmental degradation and to the challenges that come with all phases of migration.

Social norms stigmatize women who leave the safe sphere of the home to work alongside men, often in the garment factories. Sara, who had defied her family and travelled to Dhaka in triumph, explained: "I don't like working. Because people would say bad things. You know I went back home for Eid? Three girls wanted to come with me, but their parents didn't let them because people would say bad things."

I asked another young garment worker, Aisha, whether she thought her migration journey would have been different if she had been a man, not a woman. She had looked down through most of the interview. When I asked this question, she looked up at me, a terrified expression on her face. Then she looked back down and said, with emphasis, "I don't want to talk about it."

In line with Aisha's reaction, I was told several stories by women who had hidden the fact that they had moved to Dhaka to work from neighbours in the village. Others had told stories painting an exaggeratedly positive picture of life in Dhaka to cover up their actual conditions. Many earn less than expected under harsh working conditions. Arzana, a garment worker in her mid-teens, told me that she felt uncomfortable with her male neighbours but kept this to herself to avoid gaining a bad reputation:

"I don't like this. But I can't just tell this to everyone. . . . I'm scared to tell anyone because I will feel ashamed and they might say bad things about me. . . . They'll say, 'The girl has turned bad. Those boys were good before she came.'" So I'm not able to say anything.'

Listen

It became clear that female migrants faced different, and probably larger, challenges than men when migrating. At the same time, the most important thing I took away from my conversations with these women was that being vulnerable was not the same as being a victim. In other words, there is no contradiction between being vulnerable and being able to influence decisions concerning one's own life. Rather than labelling women as victims, we should acknowledge them as decision-makers in their own right. Only then can we start to fully understand both their achievements and their challenges. With increasing climate change, migration is expected to rise. If the focus is only on women who are left behind when men migrate in response to environmental degradation, the challenges of migrating women will be overlooked. We need to start listening to women's stories.

Carol Peychers

Shaping Moments

My first migration was not an overly positive one. I was a teenager when I was uprooted from Switzerland to Canada. Fifteen is a hard age to move, and I felt I missed something in growing up. Friendships were ripped apart. There was no social media, so keeping in touch was harder. Letters went unanswered after a time. It felt like a loss of connections.

Now, in my early forties, I can see some of the positive influence that first move had on me. It made me more resilient, I value family much more, and I have learned not to dwell on the past. It has made my move to New Zealand easier. I was willing to take the risk.

I arrived in New Zealand halfway through a round-the-world trip. My first marriage had failed, and I needed to get away from the tiny community in northwestern Canada where I lived. My work situation was dangerous—I received threats of gang-rape from some of the men in the small community where I worked, and I was emotionally exhausted.

The main aim of my trip was Europe. I hadn't been back since I'd left half a lifetime before. I was really looking forward to going back as an adult, but my return felt disappointingly cold, unnatural. I suppose I had changed too much.

After four months touring Europe, I moved on to Australia for a two-week visit to see family. When it was time to move on, I had a couple of possible stops left on my round-the-world ticket, and a friend was spending a year in New Zealand with her family. She was struggling with the different culture, and I thought my visit might cheer her up.

New Zealand was comfortable. The culture was halfway between Europe and North America: relaxed and open, but more structured and cultured than the towns I had lived in in Canada. My visit was only supposed to last about a month, but then I met my Mark. Mark was full of positive energy. He showed me the beauty of Fiordland and cooked amazing meals for me. He asked me to stay longer, offered to pay for a new flight home if I'd only stay an extra month so we could get to know each other.

When the month was up, Mark asked me to stay in New Zealand permanently. It was a big decision to leave Canada. Until then, I'd thought of New Zealand as a holiday, but, by then, I had learned to take risks, and I think the move to Canada in my youth gave me the courage to immigrate on my own. I flew back to Canada, sold the house and sorted out my affairs while staying with my parents for a few months. Then I said my goodbyes and flew back to New Zealand for good. I did, however, keep some money aside in case I needed to fly back—just in case.

I applied for a work permit and found work. The holiday was over, and life felt more real. I never felt trapped, though, as I knew I could go back to Canada anytime I wanted. I adapted well enough. Mark and I married and I settled into New Zealand. I tried to make it my home. However, I always had a vague sense of being isolated. Little things threw me, made me remember I wasn't at home. I noticed people often mistook my Canadian accent for an American one and weren't always friendly towards me as a result. It seemed I couldn't quite meet like-minded people in the small town I had moved to. Many of the people I knew were Mark's friends.

Most of Mark's family lived a few hundred kilometres north, in Nelson, and we went on frequent short holidays there. The climate was sunnier, warmer, by the sea. The city was bigger, the people more varied. I missed my family, and it was nice to be around his family. They included me as one of theirs. There was also work for me in my field (science), and that had become more important to me as the years passed.

After five years in New Zealand, I applied for a job in my area of expertise and we moved up to Nelson. It took a couple of years to really make friends and feel at home, but I found it much easier to meet like-minded people. Up until then, Mark had looked after everything, since he was already established when I arrived. When I moved north, I had to adapt to New Zealand all over again, in some ways. These were small adaptations, though, and it soon truly became home.

I've now lived in New Zealand for over a decade. My accent has morphed—people think I might be from Scotland or sometimes don't notice my accent.

I don't regret moving to New Zealand. I suppose I do regret leaving Switzerland—it was hard making such a huge shift at that age, and I lost touch with friends—but immigration has shaped me. I'm not sure I'd like the person I'd be if I'd never moved away from Europe, but then I wouldn't know any different.

My family says I'm too cut and dry. I don't allow emotions to complicate decisions. But I think that my life has made me more resilient, not afraid to take risks. I do shove emotions aside, yes, and that precipitates decisions, but I don't feel it's a bad thing.

I believe that it's not the town, city or country where I live that matters so much, but rather the way I view life. I think how we perceive events is more important than the events themselves, and I have learned to see the positive in whatever situation I find myself in. I live in a beautiful city with a wonderful husband, and I've made great friends. I've adapted to the culture. I'm content.

I do think Canada and New Zealand have changed me, and I am thankful for the experiences I have lived. There are moments, difficult moments, that shake you and force you to adapt and grow in a hurry. But the more resilient you are, the quicker you can move on. Any move, any migration will likely precipitate these shaping moments.

Tooba Neda Safi

Life Is a Struggle

If someone asked me to describe life in one word, I would say *struggle*. As a woman, struggling to prove your power and ability, for improvement of yourself, to get your rights, and, finally, struggling to survive.

When I think about my childhood, I see a big difference between myself and other children around the world because my childhood was full of sorrow and problems. I didn't feel free or have the freedom to play like or with other children. The reason was that war has dominated my country, Afghanistan, for the past thirty years. I grew up in the war, but the war was never the only problem that made my life that difficult or complicated. Some bad traditions and closed-minded people created a lot of barriers and blocked me on my way of life. If I wanted to progress in my life, I had to remove all these barriers in order to go on.

I was born in an educated family. My mother was a teacher, and my father was a well-educated person. They always wanted me to go to school and get a good education, just like most normal children of my age. But some of my close and distant relatives did not agree with the idea of a girl going to school. According to them, the house was better for me. They did the same thing with their own daughters.

Despite all their objections, I had the chance to go school, but there were other problems that made it more and more complicated. During eight years of my primary and secondary school, I had to suffer and go to school in dangerous situations. Our class didn't have chairs, tables, doors or windows. We sat on bare floors. Every day, we brought a piece of carpet from home in our bags. We did not have our own books in order to study. Only our teachers had books, and we had to write all the contents of the books in notebooks in order to study and prepare for exams. Sometimes I borrowed a book from my teacher, and then I didn't sleep until midnight: I copied the texts from the book into my notebook until my hand felt tired and I could not continue. At that time, there was no electricity, because of civil war, and I used to study by candlelight in the night. On top of all these difficulties, the school wasn't open all year. It would be closed for months, due to the war and security issues, which made me feel really disappointed. But, despite all these problems, I enjoyed my lessons; I made a lot of effort and always got first position in the class. In 1996, the regime changed, and the Taliban took control of the government. For years, they closed all the doors of education (primary schools, universities, etc.) and work in the faces of women and girls. The Taliban period was the worst time in my whole life. I was a teenager, and I always hoped that I could go to school again and, after that, to university and work, but all this was not possible. I stayed five long years at home, only dreaming of the day I would be able to do all that and more.

Even though there were a lot of problems and most of the Afghan girls lost hope, I did not lose the motivation and the energy to do something good in life, so I began to teach other girls in my house in the mornings and afternoons. All this was in secret; I was always afraid that the Taliban forces would find out about it. If we were caught, the punishment would be severe, simply because of our attempt to claim a right: to get educated. At times, I felt really afraid. Sometimes I had to face the opposition of other relatives who were not okay with this.

At home, we had a library. It was not that big, but it was enough, and I spent my free time in that library reading literature, history and religion (real Islamic religion, not the Taliban's religion). At that age, I began writing and started to write some pieces of poetry, but I didn't want to show my poems to anyone, because they were a mirror of my feelings, and at that time I didn't want anyone to know about what I felt. Maybe I thought no one could understand me. Radio was the only media that we had access to, and listening to the BBC was my habit. I loved all its programs, and, from that time, I decided that I would like to be a journalist.

Based on an ignorant but strict social law, I had to get married when I reached puberty, but I didn't accept. I would have considered it a failure of my life plan because after marriage it would be impossible for me to do anything. I was asked many times to marry men, but my response was always negative, and, fortunately, my father supported me and never forced me to get married. He was more than a father for me: he was a good friend, a friend who understood me and at the same time protected me. In 2001, after the long and dark five years, the Taliban regime was over. They still officially controlled some areas in Afghanistan and were secretly present everywhere, but life became, more or less, as it had been before for me.

Thank God, after those dark five years, I was able to go back to school, although, socially, the Taliban still controlled many people's mentalities. This meant I had to suffer even after I went back to school. I was in the eighth grade when the Taliban closed the schools to girls, so when I returned I had to complete three more years in order to get into university. Thanks to the efforts I had made at home in the previous five years, and the things my parents had taught me, I was able to pass the exams for two of the three years, which is possible in my country's education system. I then only had to attend the last year of high school. After I finished high school, I went to the University of Kabul and finally graduated with a bachelor's from the faculty of computer sciences. I hoped to go on and do a master's, but it was not possible at that time.

After graduation, I looked for a job. I followed my dream and got my first job with the BBC as a writer and producer. After my work with the BBC, I worked with several international organizations in the field of media and communications. This was revolutionary, as, at that time, none of my relatives had yet worked in the world of media. Again, I had to face other societal problems because of my job, but I did not really care that much about those who criticized me anymore. I felt stronger; I thought that I could bring change in my society. Deep inside me, I thought that I had a duty to work for other women as well. This is why I and a few other women made a social and cultural association, which we named Mirman Baheer; this means "The Association of Women." The aim of this association was to support women's cultural and social activities and to fight for women's rights. We published women writers' books when needed, we made workshops for them, and we tried to create some awareness-raising programs. Women in Afghanistan really needed to know their rights.

In a society like Afghanistan, it is not easy to work for the rights of women. Most of the people there say, "Woman is for house and grave." If you want to work as a woman for women in such a society, you have to be strong.

At this time, I published my novel in Pashto, *The Story Written in Eyes*. I had written it during the Taliban's time. I wanted this novel to be just like a mirror of me and other girls in our society. I narrated it from the Taliban's eyes and ideology, the way they treat and look at the woman.

My situation went on more or less the same, until I was invited, as an Afghan female writer and poet, to join a cultural workshop on Landai poetry. Normally, most Afghanis are strict, and it is not accepted for a woman or a girl to go to Europe alone. I would have liked to go to Denmark with someone because if I went with a man from my family, then it would not make such a serious problem, but it was not possible to provide a visa for a second person, since I was the only one invited to join the workshop. I wanted to introduce my culture and folk literature to young Danish students, which was the purpose of this workshop. I decided to go alone. I said to my mother that I would go for twenty days and come back quickly. This way, no one would know about my trip except for my immediate family (mother, sister and brothers). On September 25, 2014, I went to Denmark. A few days later, my relatives who were members of the Taliban became aware of my trip. I thought my trip would happen in complete secret, but it did not happen as planned. My mother called me and said, "You cannot come back to Afghanistan. You should stay there. Your life is in danger."

It was the most difficult decision of my life because I really did not want to leave my family, but I had to do it.

In Denmark, as an Afghani writer and poet, I was often interviewed by journalists, and my interviews and photos were published in print and online. This made me feel unsafe. I was also totally alone in Denmark: I had no friends and no relatives there. I was not in a situation in which I could manage my life. I was confused, and I didn't know what exactly I should do.

I had heard in the past that Switzerland had always been an independent country, that real democracy was implemented there, and that human rights in general and women's rights in particular were protected. I was under the impression that Switzerland was a country which accepted refugees, and I knew the main office of the United Nations High Commissioner for Refugees was there. I needed help and support, and I thought I might find people who would guide me in Switzerland. I also knew an Afghan family who was temporarily living there, and so I decided to go. I have been in Switzerland for two years now. I took the train from Denmark to Switzerland, and as I had a Schengen visa, I didn't face any problems entering the country.

My migrant life is not easy, and I have experienced a lot of sorrows. The problems are not over; it is only the face of them that has changed.

At the beginning, I didn't feel well, especially when I thought that I had lost my past, my future was not clear, and at that moment I was nothing. I worried about my family as well because they were under the threat and pressure of the Taliban.

I did not know what would happen next, what would be my fate. The future was unclear. It was like all the ways were covered with clouds and mist, and I had to walk and go forward.

I will never forget my first night in the refugee camp in Vallorbe, when I applied for asylum. There were sixteen beds in one room, filled with different people of different nations, languages and religions. I felt uncomfortable; I had never in my life been alone in such a strange place, among strangers. I was scared. I remember a woman beating her child. She hit his head on the wall, and he cried loudly. I put my hands over my ears and covered my face with the quilt, even though I was not able to breathe well. I could not sleep all night; I just prayed and cried slowly.

That camp looked like a prison. It was in a place near to the mountains and surrounded by trees. Away from technology (internet, computer, mobile telephone) and living among people whose identity was not clear, although most of them looked violent and ruthless, my situation made me think of movies in which a person has lost his way in a jungle and suddenly comes face to face with a strange tribe.

The food in the camp was also problematic. Because I am Muslim, I have to eat halal meat, but the meat which they prepared was not halal. The vegetables, rice and pasta were all just boiled, and I was not used to eating this kind of food. Our typical food is more oily, spicy and fried, and so I could not eat well, and most of the nights I went to sleep hungry. We were not allowed to bring food from outside, either, which is why, as each day passed, I lost more energy and felt weaker.

Another issue which was annoying me was participation in cleaning the rooms and corridors, which was obligatory. I would have liked to clean my room, but cleaning others' made me feel uncomfortable. I thought that I should work by pen, not by broom, but I had to take my turn, while tears came from my eyes. I was not given a choice.

I missed my mother and my sisters and brothers, who were in Afghanistan; I could not talk to them. My father had died in 2009, after a short battle with cancer. He was my supporter, my friend and my guide to find the right way in life, and I missed him so much. Most of the time I sat alone in my room. I did not want to talk to anyone. I was just crying, nothing else.

I stayed around eighteen days in Vallorbe. When I passed my first interview, I was transferred to another camp, which was in Neuchâtel. The type and ambiance of this camp were similar to the first one.

I still think of the Neuchâtel camp as the year nears its end and Christmas comes because I was there at Christmastime. My bed was in front of a window, and I was always looking out, like a person in prison. At that time, I almost forgot the colour of the morning and evening sun because when I looked outside, the weather was always cloudy and the mountains were covered by mist. Everything looked like a painting. All through the day, I had the same view, except for the movement of smoke coming out of the chimneys. Then I remembered the view was real and not a painting.

Psychologically I was in a bad situation, and it was getting worse day by day. In Neuchâtel, as in Vallorbe, I preferred to be alone through the daytime. I did not want to talk to other people who were staying there. When I came down to the main living room of the camp, I saw other people. Most of them were African and spoke and played together, but I sat separately and watched television. Some could speak English, but I did not want to talk. I felt comfort in my solitude. When they asked me where I came from, I replied, "Afghanistan." They murmured just three things: Al-Qaeda, Osama bin Laden and Taliban. A few of them even called me the sister of Osama bin Laden. Even though their perception about Afghanistan was not fair, I didn't care what they said because I was sure the circle of their wisdom was not big enough to realize the truth. They lacked knowledge and information. They couldn't understand me and my culture.

I had only one friend. She worked as a nurse in the camp, and her name was Anana. She was a kind girl, and when I talked to her, I felt relaxed. The social assistants were also nice people. One of them was a perfect gentleman. His name was Philippe. He was as kind as a father to me. I will never forget his kindness, and I hope God blesses him wherever he is.

I was staying in a shared room with three African girls. One was from Senegal, the second from Guinea and the last from Eritrea. I believe that when people live in the same area, especially in the same room, they have to have good relationships with each other, like a family. That's why I always tried to behave well and never disturb them, and I don't know why these girls didn't do the same.

Even though personal mobile telephones were totally not allowed inside the camp, these girls brought telephones in, hidden from security.

Normally, after dinner, I came back to my room. I prayed and read the Holy Quran, and then I tried to sleep because there was nothing more to do. I didn't even have any books in my room other than the Quran, which I had brought from Afghanistan. I could hardly avoid bad thoughts. I tried to sleep, but when my roommates came back to our room late at night, they turned on the light and made noise and woke me up. They never cared that I slept in the room. They talked and laughed loudly, and often they sang and danced as well.

When I woke up, it affected me badly, and I knew that I wouldn't be able to sleep again easily. When they turned off the light and went to their beds, they began talking on the telephone, perhaps with their friends, until around midnight. It was unbearable for me. I was not able to sleep anymore; I felt headaches and pain in the back of my neck. I just kept putting my head alternately on the pillow and under the pillow because of too much tension. I felt like I was in a grave, not a bed, and I wanted to shout loudly.

Every night was the same situation, but I still didn't want to complain about them because I thought if I did complain and reveal the secret of their telephones, it would create a problem for them as they sought asylum.

One night, I started walking around the room because I did not feel well, and the girl from Senegal asked me why I walked in the night. I said, "I cannot sleep when you are talking. You people really disturb me." She said apathetically, "This is our room as well, and we live here as we want."

I was always sad, and I felt like the world was nearing its end. I missed my family, and I worried about them because they were in danger. When anyone asked me how I was, before my tongue could say anything, my eyes gave the response with tears. I was suffering from insomnia. When the doctor examined me, he advised me to meet with a psychologist.

I was in Neuchâtel around one month, and then I was transferred to Lausanne on January 6, 2015. I started living in an Etablissement Vaudois d'Accueil des Migrants (EVAM) camp, which was located in Crissier.

The rules and regulations of this camp were better than the previous camps. Everyone was almost free, but they still didn't have normal lives, as a person could have at home. Even though, again, I had to stay in a shared room with another girl, it was all right for me because at least I could cook and prepare food by myself. I was going to French courses, and I found some friends. My roommate was a nice Syrian girl. I tried to start a bit of a normal life, then.

At the beginning, I always felt humiliated because even though in Afghanistan I had many political and security problems, I had a good position among the people. I was educated, in my society people knew me as a writer and poet, I attended many cultural affairs, I was a women's rights activist, and I worked for women in the field of culture and public awareness. I was repeatedly interviewed by many international media.

In my office, I also had a high position. I was working as a communications specialist, and I was unit head. I participated in meetings with ministers, deputy ministers, directors and managers. I had other advantages, as well. For example, I had a good salary, I was able to shop in stores and boutiques which had famous brands, and I could go to nice restaurants and ride in luxury cars. Here, everything changed, especially my lifestyle.

I saw that my time was wasting away without any achievement, and I wanted to do something good. When I rode in public buses instead of a car, when I shopped from the cheapest stores in the city and then had to carry the heavy bags from the market back to my place (which I had never done before), I felt as though I had lost my identity.

Even though nowadays the world has become like a village because it's connected with an international network through the internet and people can easily get information about different countries, about their culture and so on, when you go to another country for the first time, you will still face many cultural differences. These can sometimes be unbelievable for you.

For example, the first time I saw a girl and a boy kissing each other in public, I was shocked and I closed my eyes because I felt shame. I had watched such scenes only in Hollywood movies but not in real life; in our society, even a wife feels shy in front of her husband in sexual situations. This is why such a performance in public was not normal for me.

When I am faced with new, incredible and interesting things, I write short stories about them because I know they will also be interesting for the people who read them in Afghanistan.

I have heard from other Muslim women who are living here that when they go out with scarves, they don't feel comfortable because they face unpleasant behaviour from the people in this society. In my opinion, this is not acceptable because I think the knowledge and good character of a person set their value amongst the people— it should not matter which religion they choose. People cannot be respectable if they do not have good character.

I hoped that I could study and work in Switzerland. I would like to be an active member of the society here, as I was in Afghanistan. In the beginning, my project was to learn the French language and work as a translator. When I was staying in the EVAM camp, I cooperated with social assistants as an interpreter, since I can speak Pashto, Farsi/Dari and English.

Unfortunately, I could not continue my French courses for more than one month because of the Dublin Regulation. I came to Switzerland from another country in Europe, and, based on the Dublin Regulation, the Swiss government could order me to leave the territory of Switzerland during the following six months. The Dublin Regulation determines the country where I arrived in Europe (Denmark) as responsible for my asylum application.

The bad days restarted when the Dublin period began. I suffered a lot during this time. I had a white paper instead of a permit card, which was extended each week or twice a month. At the end of each extension, I thought that they would not extend it anymore and would force me to leave the country.

I was in a really bad situation. I was anxious and distracted. I lived in constant fear. I was even afraid when I heard ambulance sirens because I thought the police were coming and they would take me.

I didn't have enough money. My French courses had stopped. I suffered from loneliness, but I wouldn't say anything about it to my family because my mother was sick and I didn't want her to be worried about me. My family themselves were in a bad security condition and their lives were in danger; each moment it was possible that the Taliban would come to our home and hurt them.

Almost every night I had bad dreams, like someone kidnapping my brother or our house burning . . . then I woke up in fear, sweating, unable to breathe well.

I met my psychologist once or twice a week, and I explained everything to her. She finally advised me that I had to be in hospital for a while.

I did not agree to be in the hospital because the reason for my stress was obvious: I was under pressure from two sides, like a sandwich. On one side, I worried for my family, and, on the other side, I worried for my own situation, which was not clear. I was in hospital for a month. Every day I asked myself why I was there because I didn't think of myself as sick. Too many problems affected me, and my shoulders were not able to hold them anymore, but I still felt that lying on a bed in a hospital was not a solution. When I tried to leave, they encouraged me to stay and reminded me that I was somewhat protected from being expelled under the Dublin Regulation as long as I was there.

The only person who helped me a lot in this critical state was my social assistant (Pierre Amaudruz). For me, he was as kind as a father. He advised me like a teacher, and he brought my spirits up through his words like a psychologist. When I was in the hospital, he came to visit me regularly. When he gave me a small box of fruit one day, I felt like a child being given a gift by her father, and it made me happy.

Sometimes, I tried to write a poem or post some words on Facebook that reflected my feelings, but often I wouldn't even be able to write a phrase. I just sat silently, like a sculpture with no sense.

Finally, the six-month Dublin Regulation period was over, and I was able to get my Permit N back. I then passed a second interview, and, after three months, I got the result: I was accepted as a refugee and was given a political Permit B! It was the best news that I have received, after such a long time waiting. I felt happy. First, I called my mother in order to give her the good news because she had worried for me more than anyone else. When I told her about the result, I felt happiness in her voice.

At that point, I thought that my problems were finished and at last I could breathe and be a bit more relaxed, but, unfortunately, that was not the case because a new door of problems has opened in front of me.

Maybe, as a reader of this story, you think that I am a pessimistic person, but that is not true. Only if you put your feet in my shoes could you understand me.

Once I received my Permit B, I could only stay three more months in the EVAM camp before I had to find an apartment for myself. I was not able to find an apartment in this period of time, and so I had to go to a hotel.

I have now been living in a hotel for eight months. I can only sleep here. I cannot prepare food here because there is no kitchen, and I have to eat out or have takeaway food. I am suffering from anemia, and, based on medical check-ups, it is increasing and other vitamins in my body are decreasing. My doctor has advised me that I have to eat well, but for me it is not possible, and that is why I always feel weak and my blood pressure is too low.

Staying in a hotel for a few days or to spend your holiday can be joyful, but living for several months in a hotel is not easy because you cannot live as you want. You must be careful of all sorts of rules. In my case, actually, I have not been able to live as I want or as I wish since I came to Switzerland. I couldn't even decorate my own room.

At the beginning, I didn't think finding an apartment would be such a big deal, but now I realize that it is more difficult than anything else I have done up until now. I have been looking for an apartment for about a year, and I have applied for so many, with no luck. The rent will be paid by social services, but I do not have a job or someone who would be willing to act as a guarantor, so no one is willing to rent their apartment to me. I can work, and I want to have a job, but how can I find work when I can't even find a small apartment in which to live? Sometimes I asked myself why these people are so cruel. Nowadays, I am absolutely without hope. When I submit my documents to the agencies to apply for apartments, I'm just waiting for a negative response. I can't even think positively anymore.

I'm tired of everything. I can't even be motivated anymore. Even though I had many problems in my country, I still had motivation and believed that I could bring about changes because I was a young girl, I had knowledge, and I had the power to fight against the problems. But here, I do not think so.

Most of the time, physically I am here but mentally I am in Afghanistan with my family. When I hear news about any bad event or explosion in Kabul, I become worried and quickly try to call my mother. When she doesn't respond, I call my brothers and sister in a hurry, while my hands tremble and my heart pounds, until I'm sure that they are fine. I constantly fear they may be hurt.

I can't talk to my mother for a long time because when I hear her tired voice, which is full of sorrow, I feel like my heart is burning. I can do nothing for her, which always makes me feel so sorry. I really miss my family, but I don't know if I'll ever be able to see them again.

Sometimes I ask myself if I want something which is really impossible, or if I wish for something which is abnormal. I only wish for a normal life, like other people who are living in this city. I wish to have a small house and to live with my mother, brothers and sister and never be afraid of losing them. I would like to be able to massage my mother's head when she has a headache and make her happy when she is upset. I want to study and work and take responsibility for myself. This is what I hope; I do not want anything else.

In spite of all these disappointments, a small green light is still shining in a corner of my heart. It murmurs to me that one day the problems will be over, life will smile for me and it will be my day. But I don't know when.

Dr. Shruti Kapoor

Safe

It was the first time I sat on an airplane, the first time I left India. As the huge Lufthansa plane took off from Delhi for Chicago, I felt excited and intimidated. I had travelled alone many times in India, done twenty-four-hour-long journeys on the train, but nothing compared to this: a fourteen-hour direct flight which took me ten thousand miles away from my home, my country. I was comfortable, but it was all too new. I had never tied a seatbelt or crossed over the ocean to another continent. I travelled alone, with two heavy bags packed up to the brim. Who knew what I would need in a new country? My mom had used every inch of that suitcase and filled it with snacks I liked to eat, clothes that would keep me warm on those snowy days and utensils I could cook Indian food with.

Once I came out of immigration at the Chicago airport, I saw no familiar faces. I had an address book and some dollars in case I needed to use a payphone, but my aunt and uncle had assured me they would pick me up. I waited patiently for forty minutes before they showed up, having been stuck in traffic.

A few months earlier, one of my uncles who lived in the United States had come to India on holiday. I was finishing my bachelor's degree, and he suggested I came to the USA to do a master's degree. I had never intended to leave India, and I had already started the application process for an MBA there. But I was open to his suggestion, and I applied to Marquette University in Wisconsin. I soon received not only confirmation of my acceptance to pursue a master's in Applied Economics but also a scholarship.

With less than two months to prepare, I had to rush to get a visa to the United States. My father and I went to the US Embassy in Delhi. The line was really long, people looked stressed out and security was strict. Only the applicant was allowed inside, so my father waited outside. Cell phones were not allowed in. I knew that my chances of getting the visa were fifty-fifty, as a young single woman. The officer asked me a few simple questions and approved a five-year student visa right away.

Education has always been my strength and a big part of my life. My parents sent me to convent school because they felt I would get more discipline and it would be a safer environment. When the time for college or university came, I went to an all-girls college in Mumbai with onsite hostel. While safety was a big part of the choices my father made with me, within my family there was a strong focus on culture and education. Luckily, I always excelled at my studies and was a disciplined child.

I grew up in the city of Kanpur, which is famous for its leather products. When my brother and I were born, my mother chose to stop working as a teacher. My father was the sole breadwinner, and my mother focused on raising my brother and me. In India's patriarchal society, there's a clear distinction between the roles of women and men in the household. My family is close-knit, and we were six in our household: my grandparents, my parents, my brother and I. All my cousins, aunts and uncles lived within walking distance. We had enough to be comfortable, and we knew the value of money.

Like most girls and women in India, I experienced sexual harassment firsthand. Sexual harassment is common in India and other parts of the world. When I was about eight years old, a child in my family acted inappropriately playing "doctor" with me. My parents had never spoken to me about sex, and so I didn't understand what was happening. When I was a teenager, one of my father's friends groped me publicly, in my house and in his house. He was a big guy. I tried to avoid him, but I never had the courage to tell anyone. Street harassment was very common when I was growing up. Girls and women are usually given the message to walk away from, ignore or keep quiet about such incidents. There is a sense of shame and stigma associated with sexual violence.

I had travelled extensively around India before I moved to the United States, but I had never left the country. When I was eighteen, I went to study in Bombay, which was a much larger metropolitan city, almost the size of New York City. While I experienced a culture change when I left Kanpur to go to Bombay, the USA was a completely different experience. It was like nothing I had ever seen before. The USA was advanced in many ways in which I had never imagined. Everything was clean and well organized and functioned like clockwork. There was no chaos. I had to adjust and learn these new ways in the first weeks and months. I was grateful to be able to stay with my aunt and uncle for the first few weeks, and then I moved into graduate housing. I had my own apartment, and this was the first time I was truly living alone, responsible for every single thing. I had never cooked before, I had never used an ATM, and my parents had paid for my tuition in India. Now I was living completely alone and was financially independent. It was a lonely life at first. In India, there are millions and millions of people and everybody is in your face; people are everywhere. Milwaukee was anything but that. There were fewer people; everyone minded their business and was busy in their own lives. The winters were very cold. There were snowstorms and blizzards. It got dark at three in the afternoon. Some days were depressing. I didn't know how to drive, I had no roommates and I was trying to make friends. I was the only Indian in my program at the university.

International calling was still very expensive in 2000, and we didn't have WhatsApp or FaceTime. My parents called me for a few minutes once a week, and the rest of the time we wrote letters.

It took me a while to get friendly with the Americans and other Asians. I always felt like we were friends but there was something missing. The kind of connection I would have with an Indian friend was different. Their lifestyle and thinking were different.

Nevertheless, within a few months, I knew I wanted to stay in the USA. When I finished my master's two years later, I decided to settle here and find a job. I really like the education system, the lifestyle, the system as a whole. I always had the option to move back to India.

I also always knew I wanted to marry an Indian man who, like me, had been brought up in India. I worked as an economist for the World Bank in Washington, DC, for two years before I moved to California to pursue a PhD in Economics. I met my husband there. We dated for two years and then got married. Our parents approved early on in the relationship. We now have a three-year-old daughter, and I'm teaching her to speak in Hindi.

It is my hope that I will be able to raise my daughter with the same Indian values that I grew up with. Expose her to our rich Indian culture and traditions, the foods, the festivals and the beautiful country. It will be challenging living in the USA, but I will strive to do my best and leave the rest to her.

I appreciate the quality of life in the USA. I like what this country stands for, the opportunities, how an average person has access to the basics like food, water and electricity. In India, regardless of how much money you make, you're still grappling with power cuts, infrastructure, etc. With frequent power cuts in my hometown, corruption and red-tapism, day-to-day is exhausting.

With the Trump administration, politics and policy changes in the USA are making things harder for immigrants. My husband and I are on an immigrant visa, and every time we have to re-enter the country, there's always that fear of rejection. An immigration officer behind a desk at the entry point in New York can still stamp a NO and not allow me to come home. That's always there at the back of my mind.

I have lived in the USA for nineteen years now, and I've never been racially discriminated against. The only time I felt like an outsider was after my marriage. I had to come into the USA on my husband's visa as a dependant, and that prevented me from working for three years. It was an extremely frustrating period. I'm highly qualified, well educated, yet I wasn't allowed to work. Things have improved with new laws, but as long as we don't have a green card, there will be limitations.

Both my husband's and my parents are in India, and they are aging. Technology allows us to be connected every day through video calls, and I go back to India at least once a year, but we worry about the future, when our parents will need us and we'll be ten thousand miles away.

Every parent would probably like to live near his or her child, and my choice to emigrate probably saddened my parents, yet they always gave my brother and me the freedom to choose what we wanted to do in life and where we lived.

In 2012, during the period when I couldn't work because of visa limitations, a horrific gang-rape case in New Delhi shook India. I felt compelled to actively do something about girls' and women's safety, so, nearly six years ago, I started Sayfty, an organization which advocates for gender equality and speaking against violence. The whole issue of violence against women stems from the fact that women are not considered equal to men, and that's when men feel they can exert their power through violence. As long as women are perceived as second-class citizens, there will be disrespect, harassment and violence against them. The underlying cause is a patriarchal society and entrenched gender inequality. Even in the United States, a country that is so advanced and rich, gender inequality is still a problem. It's visible in work, childcare and every other aspect of our lives. I'm aware that migration often increases violence against women and girls, but Sayfty doesn't yet have the capacity to do work in that area. The sense of shame that made me keep quiet about my father's friend groping me as a teenager, this imposed shame that so many women experience around the world, is what we're trying to change in our work with Sayfty. We encourage women and girls to speak out against any form of violence.

While I live in the United States and am very happy here, I will always be an Indian at heart. I don't miss home, because this is home for me now. I do miss the people, my parents, family and friends, and wish they were closer to me. I remain very Indian in my values, likes and dislikes. I celebrate Indian festivals, love to wear Indian clothes and watch Indian movies and keep up to date with Indian current events. I think I'm a good mix of Indian traditions and values and the Western culture that I have imbibed here. I'm westernized in my ways of thinking, in how I perceive what freedom means as a woman and advocating for gender equality even though I come from a patriarchal society. I saw how gender roles were defined in India, and my views have changed: I constantly challenge these roles and stereotypes.

Laura Tam

A New Life

I was born and raised in Hong Kong, then a British colony. I received my early childhood education in a missionary school, then switched to a Christian school for my formal high school education. All the subjects were taught in English. I elected two lessons a week to learn Chinese literature and Chinese history. Looking back, I think that was a smart choice. The two Chinese courses I took in high school were counted as two credits which allowed me to get into the University of Hong Kong. My plan then was to finish a four-year bachelor's degree in Chinese History and Geography. At that time, I really wanted to become a teacher. However, I left the university after two years of intensive studies because I ran out of money to support myself. My father had lost his business, and our home was foreclosed. I was twenty years old. My older sister, who is seven years older than me, was working as a social worker with the government. She had limited means to help support her siblings. I knew then that I had to go and work. Luckily, I got a teaching job in a local private school. I had to teach seven classes from 9 AM to 1 PM, with just twenty minutes' break. Besides teaching in the morning, I also took a teaching job in the evening, from 8 PM to 10 PM. The morning-session students were young kids, while the evening students were adults who were new immigrants from China.

I also pursued secretarial training. As soon as I finished my secretarial diploma, I quit my day teaching job and found a job in a bank, working as a junior clerk. Being a bank clerk was not my plan. I wanted to find a job in an international organization that would pay me better, so that I could save enough money to pursue and finish my university education. I was eventually lucky to get a job as an administrative assistant to a management group which was under the umbrella of an international voluntary organization. My work was to coordinate and help implement the work of helping refugees from China. At that time, China was in the middle of a cultural revolution, and a lot of people fled to Hong Kong. We received funds from Europe, the United States and Canada to help the refugees' daily lives and to supplement their families' incomes until they were qualified to migrate to other countries. I got a lot of exposure to the foreigners who came to Hong Kong to pledge their support. I was so touched by their enthusiasm and kindness. Their passion to help was not found in Hong Kong. Gradually, my desire to leave Hong Kong to see other parts of the world was getting stronger. I started to budget so that I could save enough money to fly to North America.

Migration was never my dream. Coming to Canada was my destiny. I had seen a lot of Hollywood movies, read about American history and wanted to go there someday. In the fall of 1966, I decided to get a tourist visa from the American Consulate. I was rejected. I suspected the reason was "being a single young woman" who most likely would not leave the States and perhaps find a man to marry and stay. So I tried Canada. Amazingly, the Canadian Consulate welcomed me to apply for a landed immigrant visa. They acknowledged that I was young, English-speaking and well educated, with secretarial and administration skills. I got my immigration visa within six weeks. They told me that I had to land within six months. I was shocked and overwhelmed. I had not told my mom or any of my family of my plans until then. They were shocked too. My mom was shaking, since it had never occurred to her that one of her children would just go to another country to pursue a new life. My older sister and my brother-in-law were more calm. They actually encouraged me to be the pioneer and find a greener pasture. At that time, the Hong Kong people were shaken by the Chinese Cultural Revolution. They were all scared of living under the Communist regime. After a

few days, we all calmed down, and my mom and siblings all supported the idea of me being the pioneer.

Oh, how I loved the fresh air, the beautiful city, the near-noiseless
surroundings as I rode in the taxi to my temporary accommodation.
That day was April 11, 1967—my first day in Canada.

I soon made connections with a group of young women who were
like me, migrating to Canada. We were about the same age. Some
had already found jobs as flight attendants, library assistants, department store sales clerks, office clerks or nursing aids. None of
them were professionals, but they were skilled workers like me. Their
success in getting jobs gave me a boost in job-hunting. I regarded
myself as energetic, well educated and well groomed and had administrative working experience, so I felt I should have no fear of
being unemployed.

I went to the Manpower centre looking for employment.
They gave me a few tests in English, conversational and written, and
also tested my typing skills, shorthand and ability to use the newly
introduced IBM electric typewriter. I passed all the tests with high
marks. They gave me a list of companies to call and send my résumé
to. I did all that and waited for more than two weeks. Nothing happened. So I went back to the Manpower centre. They took a closer
look at my résumé and asked me a few questions, then advised me to
try the banks. I went to the big banks and handed in my application.
Still no replies. I got worried. I started to feel homesick.

Meanwhile, I saw on television the world news showing the political turmoil in China and Hong Kong. The Hong Kong people wanted
to flee to North America for fear of the Communists. Soon, I got a
telegram from my older sister. She told me that she and her husband
had already submitted an immigrant visa application to Canada! On
one hand I hoped they could join me, but on the other hand I would
still miss my mom.

I kept on trying and went for at least three job interviews a day.
The answers I got were either I was overqualified or I was lacking
Canadian work experience. I knew very well, too, that they preferred
to hire a man than a woman, they preferred to hire a local than a
new immigrant, and they preferred to have someone whose mother

tongue was English. I got frustrated. So I filled a résumé with only high school education, just seeking a clerical job, an office assistant or a bookkeeping and filing job. I even tried the stores in Chinatown. They did not even look at my résumé. They looked at me and said, "Young lady, you don't belong here. Go work in a big bank. You are not a Chinese. You don't speak our dialect." In those days, people in Chinatown all spoke the Tai Shan dialect, to which I had had no exposure while I was in Hong Kong. We speak Cantonese or a little bit of Mandarin.

I did not get angry. I forgave them. They were right. I was a Hong Kong lady, a product of colonialism. But I was a Canadian landed immigrant. I wanted to make a new life in this country. I could not give up. I prayed every night for God's help. I just needed a place to start.

Then I got a call from the CIBC, one of the big banks in Canada. They sent me to the personnel department for an interview! That day, I packed my lunch kit, all my identification documents and all my credentials to see the personnel officer. I still remember her name. She was well groomed, polite and soft-spoken. She asked me a few questions, including what my aspirations were. I drew back a little, because working in a bank was not my aspiration. So I said I needed a job to start my life in Canada. She smiled and said that I was well qualified but I had no Canadian work experience. Oh, not again, Canadian work experience! I couldn't be polite anymore. I told her what I had encountered in the past weeks of job-hunting, the people I met, the words I heard, and finally I said to her, "You can help me by giving me a job to earn Canadian experience. You won't regret it. I know my ability, my willingness to do a good job and to be a legitimate Canadian citizen." She was touched. She sent me to one of their branches to see the branch manager, who hired me right away.

It has been fifty years since I got my first job in Canada. Since then, I met my husband. With his financial resources and kind heart, I managed to sponsor my mom and my siblings to migrate to Canada. I went back to the university to finish my bachelor's degree. I gave up on the idea of going to law school. I was forty years old when I got my bachelor's degree. I chose to work part-time, to have more time to raise my boys and be a helpful wife. We have two sons, two daughters-in-law and three granddaughters. We are retirees now.

My life in Canada is filled with grace from God. This is a beautiful and free country. This is a multicultural country which offers people a chance to integrate, a chance to be respectful and love Canada.

Melissa Meza-Rapp

The Perpetual Foreigner

"You've gone native!" my friend said accusatorially to me last year when I told him I spent New Year's Eve in my pyjamas watching the ball drop on TV. To him, it was an unpardonable breach, a betrayal of my culture to not spend the last evening of the year wearing my finest clothes, with yellow underwear for good luck, eating grapes, drinking too much, with a pocket full of lentils for prosperity and toting suitcases after midnight to call forth travel for the year ahead. The reasons why I spent New Year's Eve in such a way, for the first time in my life, were of no real import. He was disappointed, and I must admit I was a bit disappointed in myself.

As an expat, the myth I wanted to believe was that I wouldn't go native. I wouldn't lose the part of myself I had when I first became an immigrant, the day I landed in the United States of America. I wanted to believe that I'd remain a genuine, true, born-and-bred Colombian and Venezuelan. I would forever bleed the colours of my flags. I wouldn't forget my roots or the land that saw me born, or the land where I grew up. I *knew* that land would always call my soul, its hold on me unbreakable, undeniable. I wanted to believe that decades of speaking a new language and learning new customs would have no impact on the core of who I was, that the identity my former home afforded me would remain there, untouched. After all, being an immigrant was the only identity I knew. I was born in Colombia and moved to Venezuela when I was barely four years old. I grew up as a Venezuelan, speaking with a Venezuelan accent, learning Venezuelan history and acting like a girl from the capital city of Caracas. I was also Colombian; it was unavoidable, unchangeable. I vacationed in Colombia at least four times a year, so I was constantly in touch with my birth nation. I danced to Colombian music and spoke with a Venezuelan accent.

When things in Venezuela, my resident country, became too hard to bear, we made the decision to move away. I dropped out of law school, and we sold everything to escape the tyranny and oppression the country was under, which has grown and worsened exponentially through the last decade. Where do you escape to when your home country is not doing well and the country you reside in isn't doing any better? I don't think we literally asked ourselves that question. I don't think we took the time to complain or rail against our fate. There was no time for philosophical discussions, only time for practical ones. We acted. We decided. We chose to leave.

My mother and I boarded a plane to come to the US, my father stayed behind, and my sister followed her dreams of Spain and Europe. Immigration and legalization would come more easily for her, without a language barrier and with her ability to almost immediately validate her law degree in Spain. Sometimes I envied the freedom she had to travel the European continent legally, while I was trapped in one state (figuratively and literally) by the burden of illegality and having no documentation.

For over five years, the core of my family was spread throughout South America, Spain and the United States. Every Christmas, every birthday, every personal celebration felt like a scab being peeled away because we were so far away from each other. We chose that over hunger, kidnapping, being killed for your car, as my childhood friend was, or getting mobbed at the supermarket for chicken, milk, sanitary napkins or toilet paper.

The curious thing is that whether a migrant comes into the new country by land, by crossing the Rio Grande, like many do, or by plane, like I did, there is one thing we all have in common: We didn't make the decision to leave lightly. Maybe the migrant is fifteen, crossing that expansive land surrounded by strangers and praying she will make it alive, so dehydrated she dry-cries, or maybe she is on an economy flight to Miami, staring at the back of the chair in front of her in a daze. We are all missing the familiar, and terrified of the unknown that awaits us.

Whether we enter this country illegally or via plane under the guise of being a tourist, our realities are all similar after the border-crossing. We are all equal in our "illegality" once our permit to stay expires. While the burden of that label never eases, it does get kind of lost in the face of everyday life. It gets put aside in the routine and the hustle and bustle of going to work, going to the gym, buying groceries, getting sick, going on vacation and just simply . . . living. Living this new life, where my former nationality, my former customs, my way of doing things gets pushed to the side to make way for how things are done here in my new country, my new home. I believe that's true even when a migrant chooses a country or community that has a rich Latin American community.

But then, no matter what, no matter how much noise, how much traffic, how much routine gets in the way of that old version of me, something always happens. I catch a whiff of home in the air, unexpectedly, like an ambush, and there it is: that version of who I used to be, at the forefront, reminding me of what used to be my home. It happened one time when I was visiting Miami, walking by a bakery. The smell of the bread catapulted me back to the time I walked to school in my ugly uniform of baby-blue polo shirt and navy-blue pleated skirt, white knee-high socks and black shoes, barely a teen. I could smell the yeasty aroma of bread, mixed with the heat of the day and the exhaust fumes of the buses. I could've sworn I smelled the scent of trees that came to the valley of Caracas from the mountains that surrounded it. Another time, I walked into someone's kitchen and the smell of Axion, a dishwashing detergent and cleaning staple of every Colombian household, kicked me in the gut. I was thrown back to a summer I spent in my aunt's house in Colombia.

It makes you wonder how a simple smell, a scent floating in the air, can rob you of your breath and remind you so strongly of that other side of you that lies dormant most of the time. How can that speck of a memory make your eyes blur with tears and your heart seize after so long?

Studies have found that there is an intrinsic relationship between smells and memories. Smell receptors are in the limbic system, which is a part of the brain that scientists call the emotional brain. That's why smell can so powerfully catapult us back to a moment in the past we thought we had forgotten. It can take us back to the memories we didn't even know we had. You never know when the limbic system will attack. Sometimes years go by without feeling that knot in your throat, and the longer you're an immigrant, the longer the periods where that duality is dormant. Then you get betrayed by the good old olfactory bulb and sent back down memory lane, where you think about the land you left behind, and your heart feels like it shrinks to half its size.

If you are one of the lucky ones and you have emigrated and found a way to "legalize" yourself and live in your new country of choice with papers and "in the light," then the experience of being an expat can be almost painless, heart shrinkage kept to a minimum and happening only when thoughts of home come barrelling down on you with no way to escape them.

If you live in the dark, however, then missing home is all you know. Being undocumented keeps you from truly belonging, from making this a home without the possibility of it all falling apart. The threat of deportation forever looms, clouding everything. You're virtually trapped by the decision you made to move to a new country. It doesn't matter what reasons brought you here. Your escape may have been politically or socioeconomically driven. Maybe you feared for your life for religious reasons; maybe you dreamed of being gay, or bi, or trans, without it meaning a probable death. Maybe it was simply a matter of needing to eat. Whatever it was, you can't go back. Living in the shadows and not belonging is better than the threat of death, starvation or civil war. You are a victim of this conscious decision to live here, and you make that decision again every single day.

There is a feeling of shame that comes with being undocumented in the United States. The first decade of my life in this, my new country, was spent struggling for documentation, trying to find a way for the system to allow me to stay. While you wait for that moment to happen, you are in the closet. You don't tell people you don't have any papers. It's a shameful secret, the crazy wife hidden in the attic. A secret cross you carry with you everywhere. You learn to live this double life, where you pretend, without saying it, that you have a right to be here. You drive around, work, rent a house, your children go to school, all with the appearance of legality. What you don't mention is the corners cut, the favours asked, the constant fear of discovery, the constant worry over what will happen next.

If you are lucky, you get hired by someone who will pay you under the table. If you're lucky, you work with fake papers, flipping burgers at the local McDonald's. If you're lucky, you won't have to stand at the local Home Depot, waiting to be hired for the day and carted off, like a work dog, on the open back of a truck for a day of backbreaking labour. It's an everyday thing, an every-second thing, non-stop, like breathing, the never-ending decision-making, the never-ending risk of doing something that will affect your entire future. The most routine of things becomes monumental. How many people get in the car each morning without a second thought? But you don't—you get in praying that nothing will happen, that a cop won't pull you over on a routine traffic stop today. Maybe there won't be an accident and there won't be a need to face what will happen for driving without a licence or insurance.

All those little mind-numbing, guilt-inducing yet necessary decisions tear at you, the worry of it all an unceasing buzz at the back of your head. It's pervasive, that fear; it's a constant, nagging, dull ache that blooms in the middle of your chest. You feel so alone, which is ridiculous since there are millions just like you. But you're not supposed to acknowledge or tell people who you are, what you are. It's a culture of silence that alienates you from others.

And still, there is time to laugh and have fun, party, fall in love, spend the money earned on furnishing an apartment someone kind enough rented under their name so you could live in it because you can't rent a property without having papers. There are milestones to celebrate, maybe having saved enough money to pay an attorney and start a path to legalization, or going up a grade on ESOL classes and understanding those around you and being understood. Sometimes it's as small as running into someone at the grocery store, saying hi and realizing you have created a network of people, friends, urban families. That small joy of being known to someone in this new place is a balm to all the hurts. Sometimes it's big, and you see the fruits of your labour enjoyed and multiplying in the home you left behind, because you have shared your blessings via money transfers.

The time spent living "in the dark" makes you miss home even more. It makes you question why you're here, it makes you yearn for that old reality, the person you used to be. It's different for those who had careers and degrees and find themselves in a new country doing menial work; they may feel humiliated by it, by the loss of prestige, by the wasted talent, knowledge and intellect. If, like me, you came in young, spoiled and reckless, then you'll miss the freedom of having it all without having to work at it.

Those are the dark days when the yearning for the land where you drew your first breath becomes a physical thing, an oppressive force that holds you down. It's more than just the shared culture, more than the familiar places and traditions that you yearn for. It's more than the familiar smells of food and holidays. It's more than the people left behind who share your blood and your history. It's more than missing the familiar landscape of mountains and beaches, or buildings and corners. It goes beyond the memories of tastes that can't be recreated. It's missing yourself *being* there. Who you were when you were there. How it shaped you, made you into the person you were before this.

When in the dark, the yearning for that self and that home can be crippling. It can make you second-guess the decision to come, no matter how bad things were before. Even with the small every-day happiness and the distractions of daily routine, the yearning is always there. Where home used to be is a hollow in your heart, and it yawns wider and wider until it threatens to swallow you whole.

Through it all, through the yearning and the pain, the shame and the fear, you fall in love. You wake up every morning with this new partner by your side. You're still getting to know each other and learning what makes each other tick, but falling in love with your new home is inevitable. You learn to love this new place, with its vast geography, haunting history and amalgamation of cultures. Slowly you embrace it, even while it doesn't embrace you back. You laugh and partake in new traditions; baffled yet charmed, you hunt for Easter eggs and learn how to bake pumpkin pie, learn to like American football, learn to call it just football. If you're lucky, you get to know this large and breathtakingly beautiful new country and feel thankful that, even hidden, shamed and in fear, you are here. Here, getting to know, making friends with, making love with, dating, marrying its citizens. Citizens that, despite some current worldwide opinions, are good, kind, curious about your country and culture, and so willing to go above and beyond to help.

Some of us will be lucky enough to have an opportunity to change, an opportunity to step forth into the light and start the process of becoming a legal immigrant and not an undocumented one. The process of legalization can be painfully dehumanizing, and throughout the whole bureaucratic, redundant, illogical, expensive, time-consuming, humiliating process you learn to suck it up, to grin and bear it. What else can you do? For some of us, at this point, we've spent years in this country and become a new entity, a combination of the person we were and the person we are now, affected by the laws, the ways, the culture of the place we now call home.

Finally stepping into the light feels like taking a breath after being held underwater. Every worry, every fear, every humiliation is suddenly erased by that cleansing gulp of fresh air. While you are undocumented, every authority figure—police, lawyer, judge, immigration agent, security guard in public buildings—everyone represents a possible threat to your way of life. Then, once you have that much-awaited green card in your pocket, it feels magically different. Their stares are friendly or flirty; they seem cordial where before their approach felt menacing. No matter how much the system made you feel like dirt, and it indeed made me feel subhuman sometimes, you forget it all, forgive it all. Maybe it's like mothers who give birth, through pain, blood, sweat and everything, and then just . . . forget! They forget how terribly painful it was, how draining on their bodies to carry that life within. As soon as that bundle of squirming baby is placed in their hands, as soon as they hug that little person who just a second ago was tearing them apart from the inside out, it all makes sense.

Some of us choose to stay there, green card in hand, a legal resident but nationality untouched. Some of us choose to go beyond and make the hard decision to become a citizen.

As you stand surrounded by people in front of immigration agents who before acted so hostile and now beam at you, you think back to those days when you didn't think it would be possible. You raise your hand and pledge allegiance and, if sentimental, you cry. Every tear a reminder of all the sacrifices that led you here. Missing family members' funerals back home because you couldn't travel outside the country. Missing weddings and happy events. Missing the career you used to have, your calloused hands clutching that tiny flag you wave with a mixture of joy and sorrow. If not sentimental, then you stand there, stoically, reciting the words, proud to become a citizen, joyful to have survived the shade, eager to walk in the light.

So, you forget. You forget how you used to be afraid of them, the immigration agents who are now smiling and shaking your hand because you are one of them. You forget how afraid you were over the seemingly unchecked power they had over you and your future. You forget about the visceral, instinctual reaction you had to their lettered forms and cold and abrupt manners. You forget how disenfranchised and alone you used to feel.

Because that baby is in your arms, and the future, it's only full of possibilities now that you belong.

During those first few days in the light, you run to do everything you couldn't do before. Get your driver's licence, buy a car, rent a house, go on a trip around the country, get on a plane to visit another city without encumbrance, do direct deposit for your pay cheque, get health insurance, all those little things so part of life, so meaningless now, yet so coveted before. You don't step out of the closet as much as kick the door down and prance out with a song and dance. You feel so patriotic, so American! Your little flag from the day of the ceremony is hanging somewhere in the house, the Constitution somewhere among your books, the letter signed by President Obama welcoming you as a new citizen maybe framed somewhere. You feel chills when you sing the anthem. You put your hand on your heart, because this land, for the past decades, during good and bad times, became your home. Your shelter.

You almost forget the taste of food as it tasted back in your old home and how the air smelled. How you used to think nothing of breaking traffic laws and now you turn your blinker on at every turn. The yearning turns into a sad ache, a throbbing that subsides a little more each day. Then you say *we* and *us* when speaking of the people in this new country. When others speak badly of Americans, you feel personally insulted, because now you're an American. You even stop being annoyed at calling it America, as if the US were the entire continent.

Life goes on, in the light. You cast your vote for the first time and feel that if they cut you, you'd bleed red, white and blue. You care about the politics of your new country, what happens to it, what people think of it, where it's going. Not only because you live in it and what happens to it will affect you but because you care, because you love.

And, then, it happens. Someone asks where you're from, and that pause . . . will it always be there? Will it go away with time? Who knows? Because the immediate answer is not "the USA." Even though you raised your hand and swore to forgo loyalty to any other country or sovereignty that you were citizen or subject to, even though you swore to defend and protect the US from all enemies, foreign and domestic, so help you God, even though that foreign enemy could be your old country, even though you meant it, with your heart and soul . . . you still pause, and your answer is, "I am American, by way of Colombia and Venezuela." Your heart is split into three.

If you're lucky, you'll get to visit your old country. In the early days of being an immigrant, you imagine your return like a movie, soundtrack and all, slow motion, revolving cameras, beautiful weather, soaring music and close-up of your tears. You'd deplane and take those first steps, and, with an audible click, your soul would find its place. Or maybe I'm just dramatic. You never thought you'd feel disconnected. Happy to be there, happy to see the family you hadn't seen in years, happy to hug them against you and feel them shake in your arms. Happy to see some things never change and some things have improved.

The thing is that you will be a perpetual foreigner, someone whose heart belongs to different lands and different people, different versions of yourself. You'll find yourself driving home on your daily commute, inexplicably and suddenly close to tears when your music player on shuffle chooses a song. The weepy sounds of the accordion will make you hurt unbearably. You will blink to stave off tears that make the green, red and yellow of the traffic lights bloom like flowers. You'll be on vacation in some faraway land, and there'll be a food truck selling arepas, and you will smile and cry. Maybe you'll choose to spend your New Year's Eve like you never have before, in your PJs, breaking every tradition, and, in your heart, you'll feel like you've lost something.

I am bound by bonds that can't be broken to that land, those people, the streets I walked on to go to school when I was fifteen, the sounds and smells of the countries that I can't forget, that I don't want to forget. The muted yearning will never go away. Some days barely ache; others are filled with breathtaking pain. A pain I have to get used to because if I left and went back to that land that still calls me, there I would just yearn and suffer for this one.

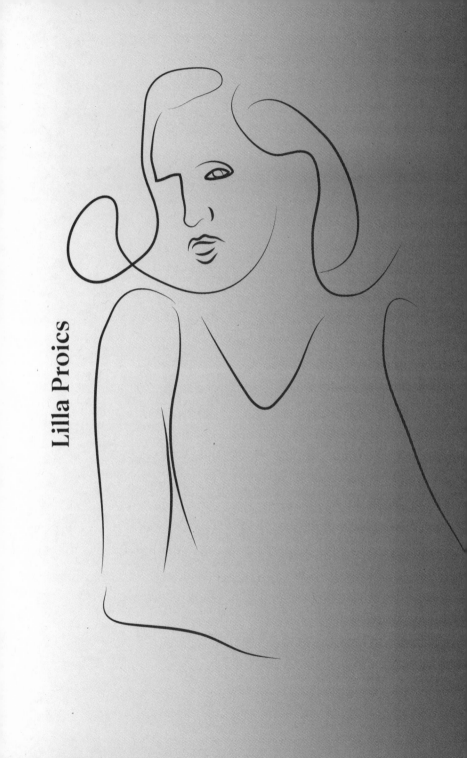

Lilla Proics

Rider

An unstoppable headache lasting for several months, triggered by an autoimmune disease, made me leave for Tiruvannamalai, India, from Budapest, Hungary.

This was my first long journey after twenty years of marriage and with two almost-grown-up children.

Then again, since my teens, I have longed to leave the place I lived in and felt tortured by the thought of being confined by the space of my life.

A little more than two months of remoteness from my own environment helped me to immerse myself in my own life, thinking it over, contemplating my problems and obstacles and how I could change the patterns that were imprinted into my everyday life. I gained a lot of inspiration for this inner journey from a Siddha healer of the same age as me. Siddha healers pass on their knowledge to their disciples, from generation to generation, over decades, adding up by now to a couple of thousand years of wisdom. It is a mindset, rather than simply healing. The strive to reach harmony in all areas of life. It encompasses your diet, how much you rest, how much you move, to what extent you are part of nature, and how much you are able to accept your environment and circumstances in every respect—the time, the space, the structure you live in—while at the same time preserving your integrity. The Siddha tradition is a verse-and song-based mythology which is transmitted orally, but they used to also write these verses and songs on palm leaves. In the healing process, they read and interpret these poems, and that is how they settle on a specific cure.

I did not experience any kind of culture shock in India. It seemed to be quite the opposite. The foods in this part of the world, for example, were the most perfect for me, and I felt blessed to walk barefoot, the way I had felt most comfortable all my life.

I relentlessly observed the local people. So many things coincided with the contemporary movement-dance arts, which I had researched beforehand. Being barefoot, for example, is a simple yet very strong sign that is used in contemporary movement and dance as well. In India, it is considered a sacred connection: to touch the ground barefoot. They work from their inner impulses, that is, far beyond individual existence. This is community or social thinking. I would rather call it an archetypical approach.

Each day, I would follow the local tradition by walking around Mount Arunachala—a walk of about fifteen kilometres—which I perceived as a meditation. The road is circular, and it leads around the sacred hill, crossing three villages and several ashrams and temples, of which the most important is in Tiruvannamalai. Basically, this temple is the religious focal point for the Vishnu pilgrims. During the November full moon, pilgrims come from every corner of the world, and for twenty-four hours literally millions walk around the road. It is an eminently theatrical experience: The crowd moves in one direction; the sacred place has to be always to their right. In the opposite direction, islands of beggars move incredibly slowly, holding strongly to each other and gathering donations. When these islands appear, the flow of the pilgrimage opens and then closes again behind them, swallowing the beggar-islands without touching them. After I walked once around, I wanted to go home to take some rest and gather more strength before taking the walk again. I had to get across the crowd to be able to walk home, which meant crossing the width of the crowd—around thirty to forty people. I started to walk across. People were incredibly close to each other, an unbelievably dense throng. Still, to my great surprise, no one touched me. And this is a characteristic of their everyday approach, proximity in the way they walk and travel. They are unbelievably close, and, still, somehow, they do not touch each other. This is how it's possible that they can move around very safely through traffic that seems like impenetrable chaos and travel without respecting any apparent rules. They proceed, organically, like the waters of the river's flow.

Because there was no electricity many hours a day, which meant I couldn't read, I started sewing. It was the first time I had sewn since I was fourteen. I made a skirt, and then a couple of smaller things, and thought back on how these household chores had been a burden to me all my adult life and how there had been expectations that I should do them. Now the burden was gone. I found joy in these simple tasks, as I had chosen them, rather than having them imposed or guilted on me.

I observed the colours around me—it is a much more colourful culture than ours. I relished the sights, the sounds, the interactions that surrounded me. I absorbed this way of life, wished to keep it with me always. Flowers are one of their basic symbols: they decorate the temples and their saints with garlands of flowers, and the ash with which they mark their foreheads is also that of burnt flowers. When they bury their dead, they carry them along the streets of the village, in a half-sitting position, and they throw flowers on the way. They step on the flowers and leave them on the streets as memories of the dead. In their different phases of blossoming and different phases of rotting, I imagine the flowers emanate very intense scents. But I cannot perceive it, as I can't smell due to my illness.

When I returned home, I was in such good shape that my whole family was astonished and baffled. They told me how much younger I seemed to be all of a sudden. I had not realized this change had taken place within me, but I did feel much better and very fresh.

After three or four months, I slipped back into the same state of numbness and exhaustion as before I had left. My younger sister started telling me that a place with a much warmer climate would be beneficial for me. Not long after, with my two children, who were twenty and sixteen years old, I left for Cairns, Australia.

My husband did not come with us. It was time to disconnect from the trapping routines, to free myself from the confinement that my life threatened to become.

My daughter attended public high school with Indigenous people; she made friends with Papuans and other islanders. When I managed to get some work, I cleaned apartments and delivered newspapers. The city has an astonishingly beautiful natural setting, and the part that was environmentally protected was of particular beauty.

I was a stranger, an outsider, a castaway in that society. But I felt free.

A couple of Hungarians, who had been Australian citizens for many years by then, helped me to get some work by putting in a good word for me. For their kindness, they asked a certain rate from me. In this way, my forty-dollar hourly wage suddenly dropped to sixteen dollars an hour.

In the end, I did not manage to get a permanent job, though I posted my CV to a couple of hundred places, platforms and forums. I advertised my skills to do cleaning or kitchen help. I went personally to most of these places, as the local people advised me to.

I delivered over two tons of coloured paper to Australian households. I drove a used car, which I rented for a fortune, as I commuted between my workplaces and my rental apartment, which was also extremely expensive. We used all the money that my mother had lent us—five million HUF, half the price of buying a flat in Budapest. My mother reminds me of this adventure whenever we meet. We went back home without a dime.

We wanted to stay, but we did not manage, as the visas seemed to be awarded after a very complicated and corrupt procedure. I never did get the promised permanent job as either a cleaning lady or a kitchen helper.

At the moment, I live in a small rental flat in Budapest with my daughter. My son lives and works in the UK.

I do not feel pressure to leave now at any cost, but, still, it could happen at any moment. It seems like a dam broke in me regarding this. I am here now, but in my mind, I managed to break free.

Karina Buikema

Coming Home

Immigrating, from my perspective today as a forty-something-year-old, seems like it should be a big deal, especially in light of the mass migrations taking place all over the world, with refugees fleeing war-torn countries. Yet, when I look back at how my immigration to Canada happened in my twenties, I didn't have the notion that I was making a big decision. I was in love, and my home country of Japan was somewhere I dearly loved but a place where I felt like I didn't fully belong, so I was eager to give my chosen country of Canada a shot. Had my immigration taken place later in my life, things might have turned out a lot differently. However, that is neither for me to know nor for you to find out. This is my story.

I grew up in a suburb of Tokyo, Japan. My parents moved there from Mexico when I was four, and I was introduced to my father's culture. I was perplexed at being repeatedly pointed out by strangers as not fully Japanese wherever I went. Yet I found my place amongst them, despite strangers' insistence that I didn't quite belong. My parents then separated at the end of my elementary school year, and my Argentinean mother moved my brother and me to central Tokyo, where she could get a job. Life was turned upside down and inside out for my brother and me. We were thrown in with strangers who didn't know us as one of them; we had to start from scratch socially. Maybe some of these moves normalized the idea of moving to Canada later on.

What those hard years following the move brought was an identity crisis: Am I Japanese or not? It is probably a near-impossible task for someone who has grown up with diversity to understand or imagine how damaging it is to stick out like a sore thumb all the time in a culture that is supposed to be yours but that you have to defend calling your own all the time, just because you're slightly different. To be assumed ignorant and excused for social faux pas seems kind on the surface, but it is a repeated cruel reminder that one doesn't truly belong. As a sensitive young adult, I had this at the forefront of my mind. As home life got tough, with my parents' separation, I craved to flee. In fact, I recall vividly praying to whatever force/power/God was out there to come get me and take me out of there. In the time that ensued, the only one that answered that call and came to me was Jesus. I became a Christian. Then, an opportunity to go to the United States as an exchange student fell in my lap, and I gleefully took it. Unlike Japan, where uniformity was celebrated, the land I was going to was one where people from all over the world gathered and made a nation; there, being different was something to be proud of. I surmised, unlike my fellow students going, that I should have no difficulty adjusting there, beyond language. After all, hadn't they always called me non-Japanese? Much to my surprise, it wasn't to be all as rosy as I had imagined. I found out then that, whether Japanese strangers liked it or not, I was quite Japanese. I experienced all the same things that other students did, including homesickness. It was eye-opening to me.

After a year in the States as an exchange student, I went back to Japan and had a reverse culture shock because I had changed. Friends distanced themselves and were perplexed by my newfound faith, even though I still considered them friends. My brother was in Canada as an exchange student, so my father suggested I also go there for college. He didn't need to ask me twice. As I went back and forth during my college and university years, I would experience reverse culture shock over and over again, and I found it took me longer and longer to readjust whenever I got back from Japan to university in Canada. When I figured out that was the reason I was performing poorly on mid-terms, I decided not to go back in the summer to Japan. Soon after that decision, I met my husband.

Within a year, we were married and my application for landed immigrant status was sent. The year was 1994.

Immigration Canada is the only government agency that does not have a civic panel or third-party watchdog. It makes its decision as it pleases, whenever it pleases. I was in love, newly married and excited about starting life with my husband in Canada. Little did I know that Immigration would file my application amongst the torrent of incoming Hong Kong immigrants'. I had heard people jokingly call Vancouver "Hong-couver," due to the onrush of immigrants fleeing the return of Hong Kong to China, but that had just been a piece of trivia to me. I didn't realize it would affect my life so much. I was advised that the process should take less than a year, since I had married a Canadian, so I was optimistically waiting. We didn't hear from them for over half a year, and when we did, they wanted me to submit a criminal-record check from Hong Kong! I'm sure my face was something to behold. We were puzzled. I've never set foot in Hong Kong! Nor am I related to any Chinese or British. How could this be logical? We called the Immigration Canada information line repeatedly and pointed out this fact, yet there was no change or reason. They parroted the same thing back to us over and over again, saying my application would remain in process until I could provide the criminal-record check from Hong Kong. Much to our consternation and frustration, the application was stymied, and time kept marching on.

Over a year had passed, and my student visa was nearing its end. I couldn't work because my application was still on hold. As university students and newlyweds, this was hard. Then a friend suggested we approach our local Member of Parliament. Ours happened to be a very prominent rookie in Ottawa, Keith Martin. We called his office and made an appointment to see him. Canada, similarly to the United States, is made up of people from all over the world. Dr. Martin himself was no exception. He was very sympathetic and promised to look into it on our behalf. That was the turning point. Within a month, we received a letter from Immigration saying that my application had been moved to the next process centre. I had applied for a working permit, just in case. The day after we received the permit, we also received my permanent residency.

From that day I have called Canada my home, and I have lived here longer than I've lived in Japan. I've met numerous people like myself who have made the leap and immigrated to Canada. All have unique stories, like my own, and it is always interesting hearing them. Generally, all love to swap stories of how we came to Canada and what fun "adjusting to Canadian society" incidents we've had. My reasons for immigrating were not born out of danger and urgency, yet the adjustment is something that we all have in common. Mine is an organic, logical path born out of an opportunity to start anew with a loved one. Leaving social frustrations behind was more a happy by-product of that decision than a motivation. This path has led me to a fulfilling place where I can grow in my faith without ridicule (okay, maybe some people still do ridicule me, but not nearly to the same extent), a country where diversity is celebrated instead of shunned, and a thriving community where my husband and I can raise our family together.

In 2009, my husband and I took our two children on an adventure in Japan. We caught the adventure fever after we sold our house. We bought an RV to come home to and set off on an epic adventure to Japan. I love the countryside of Japan more than I do the cities, and I wanted my children to see the environment in which I grew up and to know their heritage, so we did a farm stay through WWOOF (Willing Workers on Organic Farms). We stayed for nearly a year, and my third child was born there. We made friends all over, and the children even got to experience school life while we stayed in Nagano. What surprised me was the return. I was sad to leave Japan, as always. A piece of me unarguably still lives there. Yet, nearly nine hours later, when we approached Vancouver Airport, an unbelievable rush of homecoming came over me. I hadn't even realized until my whole body relaxed and I knew so clearly: yes, Canada has indeed become my home.

Hiba Dabbah Al Jamal

Journey from Death to Life

A small truck carried us, all piled up—women, men, children—like merchandise. We arrived at the meeting place, far from the eyes of the border guards. We slipped on life jackets and climbed into the boat. It had a capacity of fifteen people, not more, but the smugglers' greed pushed them to overfill the boat. We were forty-five people, fifteen of which were children. In the night that enfolded us, we heard the violent surf of the waves in the distance. We stayed hidden in the scrubland on the riverbank for interminable hours before we set off to our destination. Aboard, we delivered our fate to God and to the sea. Midway, the boat stopped. We had run out of fuel. The waves slapped aggressively against the boat and splashed us with salty water; the women and the children shouted out in fear and some screamed, but no one moved out of fear of unbalancing the boat. We added fuel from a jerry can and set off again. Everyone began to pray and implore the heavens to help us arrive safe and sound. The engine stalled again a few dozen metres from the shore. The young men on the boat jumped into the shallow water and pulled the boat on to firm land. I thought, *We've finally arrived*, but we weren't on the right island. It was desert. Shaking and terrified, we lay on the ground in our wet clothes. The cold gnawed at our limbs.

In life, each of us must make a choice: to be or not to be. Of course, it's always easy to say but not to do. I was a person among millions of others. I lived through and knew war; war is the fight that each civilian leads to survive and resist the imminent death that watches him at each instant. To live is to defeat death. It's the victory of the will over resignation. I wish to describe objectively and faithfully with as much neutrality as possible my point of view on the war in my country of Syria.

I'm twenty-three years old, but in my mind I feel much older. At least thirty.

Maybe it's the overwhelming immensity and atrocities of the events that make us mature early. Or perhaps it's despair. Of course, it's not only age that allows us to be sure of our choices; the choices themselves and their consequences sometimes make us lose the notion of our real age. For me, for others, for anyone.

What I longed for happened: to leave this war-ridden country. But was I prepared to change everything about my life? It's the most important question, and yet I didn't have the power to answer it. I let my destiny create all that has happened. I was incapable of taking any decision.

The war in my country is not a political war, as has been announced by the media, but a war against humanity, a civil war.

Those who say the dead and the victims in this detestable war are only politicians are wrong. Where do the numerous civilian graves that keep filling improvised cemeteries in small city parks and gardens come from, then?

There's no doubt these are the graves of innocent civilians who suffered harsh and unbearable conditions through years of war. I was a young woman among them; we had to endure daily hunger and thirst, and the cold of winters with no heating.

In winter, it was difficult to live in our apartments. Some apartments were devastated and practically uninhabitable, repaired with makeshift plastic sheets or bed linens. Others couldn't be heated because of a lack of wood or fuel. Soldiers were also served first.

After losing their jobs, some inhabitants had neither revenue nor food reserves. Some tradespeople increased the price of commodities, without taking into account those who had already lost everything. We didn't eat meat anymore, since it was too expensive. We ate vegetables and bread, when we could find some.

Each morning, the fathers had to go to work without being sure of returning safely in the evening. Mothers were frightened for their children who still went to school.

I remember witnessing, at the end of a school day, a bombing which killed and injured students. I heard the parents' screams as they came to pick up their children from school.

I often met children, alone, who'd lost their parents. They told me of their desire to find them again in heaven and of their sadness over not having them by their side and having to continue life without them.

What makes me sad is that childhood isn't possible in Syria anymore. Even the concept of youth has lost meaning. Life over there is simply not a life anymore.

Despite all that went on, death remains the only thing we never understand. This is especially the case regarding what happened on January 15, 2012: the carnage of the students of the University of Aleppo. It was the first day of exams. We'd barely begun when a terrible explosion shook the university's premises. The students were piled on the floor, one on top of the other, some injured and shredded, others dead. Some remained standing, petrified and stuck like nails in front of the horror of the spectacle. They couldn't believe what they saw. Perhaps they wondered if it was a nightmare or reality. That day, instead of receiving good notes on our exams, we received death certificates. In fact, I'm perhaps wrong to say "that day," as every day became like that one in my country. The only difference is that, that time, I was there, and witnessing it shook me deeply.

University was, for many of the youth, the only hope that was worth fighting for. It was also an opportunity for the boys to delay their conscription to the military service, which they could do as long as they were students. It's true that military service is a national duty, but in this war, we don't know whom to make war against, whom to turn our weapons on. I spent three years at this university. They were the best years of my life. For me, it was an adventure. It wasn't easy to be accepted to this university. It was a dream and a challenge at the same time. (I find myself in a similar situation now in Switzerland, as I'm about to pursue my studies at the University of Geneva.)

Going out of our homes at this point in this absurd war was a confrontation with an unknown fate. So, we youth had decided to defy death and fight by science and intellectual conscience against all the obscurantism that the so-called Islamist extremists wanted to impose in the name of liberty. We went to university to educate ourselves, even though there was a victim or a student each day who carried the side effects of war in the form of a mutilated arm or leg—memories inscribed on their bodies.

I miss the benches of our education. They were witness to our existence and our passage in these places. I also miss the coffees with classmates, as well as the collective laughter to forget our common pain. I miss my professors. I admire them immensely. With us, they defied these unbearable circumstances by staying there to ensure our education, despite the promising temptations to emigrate to other countries' universities, opportunities that promised them fantastic futures.

At home, in the streets, at school, death became a normal part of our daily life. How did we get here? Scenes of death and horror are indescribable and beyond all expression of indignation. However, we must say with all frankness that we are a brave people that don't surrender easily in front of the woes of life. We are ready to fight for survival, to find food to stay alive. We deserve to go down in history for our struggle.

Yes, death in Syria has become something usual. It has become the reflected image of the general state of the country. Each one of us is used to receiving bad news, such as the death of a loved one or a friend. Worse even is witnessing attacks, explosions. These horrors traumatize the depths of our souls in a painful and horrible way. We are at any moment subject to witnessing horror scenes that shake our senses and our memories. We walk in the streets and suddenly an explosion rings out from an unknown source. Dozens of dead and injured are strewn on the sidewalk. First aiders quickly evacuate the injured to hospitals, and life goes on as if nothing happened.

What was not normal for me was what happened on the damned day of September 13, 2015. Armed men that had joined the army out of opportunism managed to introduce themselves into one of my father's friends' stores. They intended to steal merchandise. My father opposed them, and a dispute ensued. It degenerated violently and ended up in a bloodbath. I've often seen these types of people falsely pretend to be patriots and to defend the interests of the country, but in fact they're ready to sell it for a few drugs or alcohol. About twenty of these false patriots rushed at my brother and my father with butcher's tools. You can't imagine what I felt that day. The scene remains lucidly alive in my mind. I can't say more about this, as since that moment, I've hated the meaning of telling the truth. If telling the truth can cause so much harm, then what can I say of evil?

A phone call marked the beginning of my departure. It was fate that would remove the rhythm of my trying routine. That day, I drank my usual morning coffee. The sun shone with intensity, as if it prepared me for some surprise. I was at work with my boss, who was also my uncle. As always, we took many phone calls from clients, but this call was from my mum. She phoned to inform me of my family's decision. It was as if they had all forgotten that I, too, was part of this family and that before taking such a decision, my parents should have also checked with me. The decision had been taken, and I was to make the journey with them three days later. At first, I laughed. Then I cried silently, so as not to attract anyone's attention. A trip abroad had always been my dream, but not under these conditions. The first thing that saddened me was that I was forced to leave my best friends, my neighbours, my studies (which were unfinished), our house and all my memories from birth to that time. At the end of the day, I cried as I walked down the street towards home. I looked at my neighbourhood as if it were the last time I'd ever see it.

I felt a deep pain as I looked at the faces around me. They seemed to all say, "Goodbye. Have a good trip, with no return." I felt as though the end of the world had come. I felt weak and beaten. That night, I assembled all my belongings: my clothes, my books, my souvenirs.

As I prepared the family's things, I sorted everything by labelled piles according to whose luggage they would go into. My mother and a close friend helped me. We laughed a lot, but we cried more as each passing minute reminded us of the imminent journey "from death to death," as this trip is often called, since so many die making it.

The following day, I took a bit of time to see a few friends for the last time. Finally, the departure day arrived. It was a Saturday. I awoke early and wondered, *Am I really about to leave my country, or am I dreaming?* I still ask myself that question.

At seven, we were all ready to leave. My uncle took us to the Pullman Road Station.

At nine, we climbed on to a bus that headed towards Lebanon. After a long trek on barricaded roads, where military harassed the passengers, we finally arrived at the Lebanese border at seven in the evening. There were also many other passengers from other buses. To take a boat and continue our road to Turkey, we had to wait for several hours. We finally boarded the boat at two in the morning.

It was cold, and the boat was normally used to transport merchandise and not passengers like us. The trip seemed to take an eternity. We could only see the never-ending horizon and the sad faces of other uprooted passengers.

At the end of the day, we arrived in a Turkish port, where we boarded a bus to go to Izmir. The road was again long and tiring. We felt like exhausted victims who didn't have the strength to object to our fate. Finally, we arrived at our destination, mid-afternoon the following day. We stayed in Izmir for nearly a week while we waited for the sea to calm itself, since it was the start of the big spring tides. It was too risky to attempt the crossing in the Zodiac boat from Turkey to Greece as long as the sea wasn't calm.

On October 26, we finally made the journey. Initially, we landed at the wrong spot, in pitch blackness. At daybreak, we searched for the right destination. Some fishermen took us part of the way, and then we walked for four hours. Finally, we arrived at the Greek border guards and they loaded us on to a ferry to Athens. There, our adventure began on firm land, with thousands and thousands of kilometres on trains and buses. From Athens, through Macedonia, Serbia, Croatia, Slovenia, Austria, Germany and finally to Switzerland. We left each country early in the morning and stopped at midnight. The cold pierced our bodies, weakened by fatigue and the desperation to see our trouble come to an end. I looked around me as if I were a fugitive criminal. The police forces were reinforced everywhere in Europe. Thankfully, we arrived safely at our destination of Switzerland, and our journey changed its name from "journey from death to death" to "journey from death to life, from injustice to peace."

My integration into this new world hasn't been easy for me, but what helped me is the kindness and respect of the Swiss community. I think my willingness and perseverance also had a determining role in the success of this adventure.

Now, I'm happy to be in Switzerland, even though at first it was not my wish, or that of my family, to come here. I have faith in God. In other words, I believe it was God's will to uproot us from a painful and unjust life, to take us far from the war and the death that watched us at every corner in the city of Aleppo.

Before the outbreak of war, life was peaceful and everything had a distinctly pleasant taste. We lacked nothing. We had our ancient civilization, our rituals, a peaceful cohabitation between all faiths. I remain strongly attached to this lifestyle; I feel that social communication and solidarity between all members of society couldn't exist in the same way anywhere else. I'm still proud that the war hasn't managed, even with everything it has destroyed, to destroy the links that unify us nationals of the same country.

I always dreamed of making good plans for my future. I think of it still, despite the difficulties. Before, in Syria, one of my great difficulties was the frustration caused by certain people who said I had too much ambition and not enough ability. I don't understand these people—is it wrong to make real plans for my life and count only on myself? And if I don't deserve to look after myself well, then who deserves to have me fight for them? No one.

I don't allow anyone to bother me anymore. I've decided to forget all that has happened because I love life.

I'm surrounded by nice, kind people who encourage me and help me continue my difficult journey, which demands effort and patience. These people are enriching, and they bring treasures of good self-esteem and improvement to me.

I have faith in my destiny, thanks to God.

Two years have passed since I began writing this story. In these two years, my world has been shaken again. More than I ever thought possible. Perhaps the weight of all these previous events caught up to me after all. The trigger should probably have been a small obstacle, but to me, then, it was insurmountable.

I attended the University of Geneva as planned. After working hard and passing the exams at the end of the first semester, I was notified that the university didn't accept the diploma which had qualified me for entrance. I was not welcome to pursue my studies there after all. My world crumbled around me—the false hope felt unbearable. If only they'd told me sooner, it wouldn't have been as devastating. I retreated and stayed home for weeks, months. I barely went out. What was the point? I felt as though I had no future. My mind gradually saw only black.

Depressed and isolated, I tried to commit suicide.

The pills didn't work, though, and I found myself in hospital under psychiatric care. I convinced the hospital staff to tell my family that I had mixed too many migraine pills and had an adverse reaction. To this day, I haven't told them what really happened. My psychiatrist encouraged me to find goals, to get back into life routines. He urged me to start at zero, like other people. He told me I was young, I had a lot to live for. He helped me a lot. Little by little, I took a new rhythm and came out of this sad period. I put a plan in my head to succeed and made progress. I thought back over my experience, qualifications and possibilities.

I decided to get a dental assistant apprenticeship that would lead to a diploma, since I had worked in that field for three years in Syria. At first, I received only negative letters back from my applications. After a while, I understood why: on my résumé, I had put a photo of myself wearing a head veil. It seemed to not be acceptable in the workforce in Switzerland. This posed a big problem for me, because I am a Muslim, and there are customs and traditions that expect me to wear a veil. It stressed me again, made me so sad. That was a fragile time. I suffered intensely, secretly. The sadness grew as it hid within me. In our culture and mentality, it's important to respect certain things. Also, my decision always belongs in part to my family.

I fought a long time to not let go. I consulted my family and my friends, as well. In the end, I took the difficult decision to accept the ways of life here and remove my veil. I was no longer in Syria but in Switzerland, and the situation isn't the same anymore at all. I feel it's important for me to earn a living and be part of the society in which I live. It was a decision that I felt would save my life, my future. This decision wasn't acceptable to my family at the start, and this caused many problems for me. Some said I was going to abandon my religion, that I would lose my faith, but they were wrong. I'm an open person, but it's not always easy because I have the burden and responsibility of explaining and justifying my actions to my family. That's how it works in my culture. We can't do what we want, as we want, without saying anything. We have to at least consult our parents.

I was willing to take off my veil during work hours. With that in mind, I changed my profile. I put a photo on my résumé without the veil and started to look for an apprenticeship position again. Thankfully, I soon received a positive response. I found a wonderful place in Sion, where I work with a great team. They've been very helpful and are always by my side. They help me with my studies and my work. I feel really lucky to work with them. I wear my veil on my way to work, remove it during work hours, and wear it again after work. I'm partway through my first year now. It will take two years to complete the diploma. Soon after I got the apprenticeship, I also became engaged! My fiancé is kind, and I feel like I live in a rosy world now. These hard memories are fading. Things didn't always go the way I would have liked, but it is what it is. It is life. I'm happy now.

I would like to thank my uncle for his immense availability and encouragement all along my journey, for his precious help and time in helping me write this essay, and for his unwavering good mood.

Tina Kreitmayr

Looking for Home

It is probably fair to say that I was born in a paradisiacal kind of place. Almost Astrid Lindgren kind of perfect—minus the long walk to school and the solitude during the winter months.

I grew up in a small town in the southwest of Germany. A river runs through it, and it's nestled among hills covered with seemingly endless forests. The skyline of the town is dominated by two steeples; one belongs to the Protestant and the other to the Catholic church, but no one ever cared whether or not you went to either one of them. To this day, the high street is a charming mix of bakeries, butchers, pharmacies, a bookshop, a flower shop, banks and hairdressers. The only thing that has really changed through the last thirty years is the extended opening hours. Most of the other buildings in this place are family homes with gardens in front or in the back.

This illusion-like idyll of timbered houses is completed by the proximity to the next city, which has flourishing automobile and mechanical engineering industries and is one of the most powerful and economically important cities in Germany and Europe. Within a thirty-five-minute drive, you can find shops, clubs, restaurants of every culinary background and, most importantly, jobs.

Throughout my teenage years, *unemployment* was a very theoretical word. No one I knew was unemployed. Most households had either a double income or one of two partners who deliberately stayed at home. It seemed both choices were equally acceptable, and having both partners work really was a choice and not a necessity to survive. The second income basically determined whether or not you could afford a second family vacation or a second car.

However, the thing that makes this place so great is something I really learned to appreciate much later. I was born in the late '80s and was, therefore, one of the lucky generation who was not affected by the war or any other major crisis. All my grandparents were part of Nazi Germany and the war. My parents were, at least during their childhood, still affected by the rebuilding of the country and later by far-left terrorism (RAF), nationally, or the Cold War, on an international level. By the time I was two, the Cold War was officially over and the Berlin Wall had been torn down. The European Union also expanded, and, eventually, there were no borders anymore.

The first time I realized that war was not just something you read about in history books was after 9/11, the start of the Iraq War. To this day, I'm more than grateful to have had a childhood not knowing what death, killing, suffering and starving meant.

My grandmother knew what all these things meant. She was born in a small town in East Prussia in 1923. Her father and older brothers fought and died during the Second World War. Like many, they were forced to participate in a war they did not believe in and to fight men from other nations with whom, under different circumstances, they could have been friends. Eventually, they were killed somewhere in Russia in 1943. My grandmother, her mother and her little brother would never know what really happened.

The areas east of the Soviet Zone of Occupation, mainly Eastern Prussia, Western Prussia and Silesia, were handed over to Poland because of the 1945 Potsdam Agreement. The German population fled, mostly to the western zones, or was driven out once the Red Army got into their towns. My grandmother was one of the "lucky" ones who got on to one of the last regular trains to the west. Many others had to flee by foot, and many died trying to cross the borders by walking on the frozen Baltic Sea. However, in this context, "lucky" is describing the mere state of surviving. She had nothing on her but the clothes she wore. Her sister-in-law and her three young children accompanied her. In the chaos in the train station and on the train, they lost sight of the youngest, a little three-year-old boy. They never found him again, despite a huge effort during that night, the weeks after and every day until they died. This was a fate shared by many others—books were written and movies were made about this type of situation—but my grandmother never forgave herself for not paying more attention.

My grandparents met while my grandmother still lived in a refugee camp, close to where I was born. My grandfather was a police officer in the very beginning of his career, and money was scarce. They moved into a small flat, and my grandmother refused to move ever again. They could have afforded a bigger place soon after, but she would not even consider looking at other places. She never got tired of telling us how important a home is, how necessary roots are, and that you need to hold tight the people you love.

Why am I telling you all this? Because this is who I am, and this is also a lot of the DNA I have received. On the one hand, I was allowed to grow up in one of the greatest places on earth. On the other hand, I learned and understood the importance of home and family early on.

And yet, I turned out to be an emotional migrant who might never be able to call a place my home.

I'm not exactly sure when it started, but it must have been sometime during my teenage years. Frankly, I cannot even recall if it happened overnight or if it was a process that lasted weeks or years. However, I can describe the feeling I was left with.

It's like being homesick for a place you have never been to and you do not know. It's like being in love with a person who feels very real but was never in your life. It's like craving a dish that you have not seen on a menu before. It leaves you restless and at times a bit envious when others talk about building houses, marrying the love of their lives or how they just had the best spaghetti parmigiana ever.

I finally packed my bags for the first time after high school. However, that was not exceptional, as half of my friends went abroad for a year off. I had the amazing opportunity to work in a school for adult refugees and immigrants in Norway. The format of the school was twofold: Norwegian classes in the morning and practical lessons for potential jobs in the afternoon. There was a kitchen, a garage and a fully equipped tailor shop. Additionally, the school offered art classes and physical activities. My job was to support the PE teacher during the indoor and outdoor activities.

On my very first day, I introduced myself to the class: "Hi, my name is Tina, and I am from Germany—"

A Somalian woman interrupted: "Is there war in Germany, too?"

"No!"

An Ethiopian woman followed: "So, little food in Germany?"

I looked at them and felt so much smaller and less enthusiastic than before. "No, I am here only for a year. I am a volunteer."

A tall Nigerian lady joined in: "You saying, you are coming here voluntarily . . . in a country with no sun, tasteless food and no pay? That does not make any sense . . . sounds like a stupid idea!"

I was not exactly stupid, but, without a doubt, I was clueless. The other women in this group were more concerned about my husband and children. When they learned that I had neither and that I wasn't planning on getting any soon, and that my parents were okay with this, the lack of mutual understanding was obvious. We spent a lot of time together that year, and I was able to learn a lot from these men and women. Until the very end of my time there, I was not able to make them understand why I would leave a safe place and go somewhere to work for free. However, I gained a whole new perspective and appreciation of safety, freedom, peace, family and home.

In retrospect, I was very happy that year. I was carefree, with hardly any responsibilities. For the first time in my life, I fell in love, and the little red house I was living in felt good, like I belonged there. I gained ten kilos, because the beer and pizza up there just tasted like heaven. When the year was over, I was truly heartbroken. The "love of my life" moved back to Australia, the house was occupied by new volunteers, and my mum picked me up at the airport saying, "Oh, wow, you got so fat!"

I sometimes wonder if the reason I was that happy was because I knew time was limited and I made the best of it. Or maybe it was because the whole year was a sequence of positive but extreme situations, and I was constantly on adrenaline. Either way, I'm glad I experienced it, because the chances I will feel that carefree ever again are rather small.

I went back to Germany for many reasons. First of all, I thought, with my newly gained appreciation of home, I'd be ready to live there again. Second, Germany does have one of the best education systems, and students do not pay any fees to go to university.

I really enjoyed my time as a student. Whenever there were no lectures, I went for great trips, and I did a couple of internships around Germany. Frankly, I did not spend more than three months in one place during these years. Although I was restless and always looking for new opportunities, I never felt lost.

After graduation, I got a great offer from a company very close to the little town where I was raised. I realized that I had been away a lot during the previous four years, and I decided to take the job. In the beginning, it was great to be around friends and family more often. Almost all of them had moved back after graduation, and our group of friends from high school was united again.

It lasted for about a year before the feeling of not being at the right place or at the right time grew strong again. And while I was truly happy to see everyone around me nesting, frustration grew in me as I wondered why I could not—did not—want to. I tried being in a relationship, but with every day it lasted, I felt more chained. I hate to surrender, so I tried hard to make this mission of "I am home" work. I could not.

After three years, I quit my job, packed my bags and decided to finally get a post-grad degree in Organization Studies. I moved to the UK and went to university there. Knowing that it was only a temporary thing, by its nature, I felt no pressure to make the UK my home. By far the oldest student in my program, I was suddenly faced with rounds of truth or dare and beer pong. This time, I was not as heartbroken when the year was over. But this time, for the very first time in my life, I had no idea what to do next.

I got back to Germany in September 2015. The refugee crisis was the dominating topic in the news, and I was very curious about the situation in the southern German countryside. I had heard all the great stories about public engagement in Berlin and Munich, but I did not quite know what to expect in the town where I grew up. I knew that the city had welcomed 450 refugees, all men, who were living in two community halls.

Of course, there were concerns among the locals. People were worried about the change, and in the very beginning rumours spread that were not helping. For example, at some point everybody was sure that an all-male refugee camp was going to be built on the grounds next to the elementary school. However, this was never even up for discussion, according to local council members, as there were existing empty buildings that were more suitable.

Time passed, crime rates didn't go up, and no one lost their job to a refugee. That is how the neighbour's new haircut once again became a more interesting topic of discussion.

I had my first encounter with our town's refugees my first night back, when I walked past the city hall on my way to my house. Around twenty men were sitting on the stairs in front of the building, busy with their mobile phones. Apparently, this was the only spot with free Wi-Fi in the entire city. Most of them spoke quietly, and it seemed like they were just boys being told by their mums to wear warmer jackets. It was cold, and they probably should have worn warmer jackets.

About a week later, I did some research on how to get involved and was pretty surprised. An initiative was founded with almost 1,500 volunteers, trying to provide a warm welcome and basic supplies. In cooperation with the local German Red Cross, many projects were established in order to make the long and nerve-racking asylum procedure as pleasant as possible.

A couple of days later, I got the chance to visit one refugee accommodation. I was welcomed with a cup of coffee and a challenging table-soccer match. The atmosphere was pretty relaxed, and alongside the forty-eight refugees, about thirty locals sat in front of the building, chatting and having a good time together. I got to know a group of Syrians and Pakistanis who were motivated and willing to learn more German; the coordinators and I agreed to establish a further language class. I started working with five young men once a week, but we were soon a group of twelve, meeting at least two or three times a week.

After a few weeks, we talked about how we pictured our futures. Most of the men would actually have loved to go back home, but considering the circumstances, they were hoping to be reunited with their families and start a safe life in Germany. They asked me what I planned to do, and I told them that I was applying for jobs pretty much everywhere except in my hometown. One Syrian looked at me and asked, "Why would you want to leave paradise?"

Although I was not too surprised by the question anymore, I still wasn't able to provide a comprehensive answer.

In the following year, I worked on different projects on the Greek island of Lesvos, in Gaziantep (Turkey) and in Afghanistan. I also lived in Zurich, Athens and London. It was a fulfilling time. I met the most interesting people, heard powerful stories and learned once more how lucky I was. Most projects took place in the context of the refugee crisis—some were paid, some were not.

In Athens, I had the chance to work in a refugee camp located in the former airport of Ellinikon. Arriving there on my first day was one of the most surreal things I've ever experienced. Just seeing the old airport building suggested the usual feeling of freedom and vacation. Seeing the people inside and outside the building caused the exact opposite emotions. I entered at the former arrival gates. On the wall was the board on which the arrival of the flight from Santorini at 11:25 was still noted. Whereas this area served as offices for the organizations on site, the departure area was filled with little tents. There was hardly any space between the tents, which were made for two people but now provided homes for families of up to five people. Outside, the temperature was about forty-five degrees Celsius (it was July 2016), and it was even warmer inside.

Part of my job was to sort donated clothes to give out to the families in Ellinikon. The entire basketball arena from the 2004 Olympic Games (located next to Ellinikon) was filled with boxes of donations. Most things I unpacked were winter jackets, woollen sweaters and scarves. A lot of other items were short skirts, shorts and t-shirts with prints saying things like "Sexy bitch" or "Drunk is always better." None was too helpful in this situation.

It felt good to work on all these different projects, but I knew that I would not be able to get any rest continuing this way. Plus, my bank account began to dry out at some point (Zurich and London didn't help). My family always supported me emotionally in what I did, but ever since high school I had tried to stay financially independent.

There was no way I would change that now, and so I decided to get back into solid employment status. Three months ago, I moved to a new city in western Germany. I'm enjoying getting to know the place and the people. The job is interesting, and, frankly, it's great not to sleep in a different bed every second week. I feel comfortable.

Will I call it home? I guess I have to wait and see.

I was born in a paradisiacal kind of place, and, just by birth, I was given the best conditions possible. I am very grateful for this, and that's why I want to make a small contribution and help those who were forced to leave their homes and families. Personally, I was never really looking for the big adventure. I don't need to move far away or to exotic places, but as long as I have not found the place I call my own home, I will be looking for it.

Anna Leuba

Motherland

My name is Anna. I am twenty-eight years old, and I am originally from Ukraine. I am married to a Swiss man, which is why I've been living in Switzerland for the last six years. In the course of this time, I studied at university and tried to work in a few areas. My personal story might be quite similar to Cinderella's: a young girl from a poor country falls in love with a prince who takes her to his kingdom and changes her life forever. Of course, my husband has nothing in common with the royal family, and Neuchâtel, the city we are living in, is not a fairy place. Nonetheless, the day we met has unalterably changed my life and divided it into the period before our marriage and after it.

Before

I was born in a small Ukrainian town in the Poltava region, which is the central part of Ukraine. My parents are divorced, and I have never really known my father. If you have ever been to any post-Soviet country, you know that a high rate of divorces and a large number of incomplete families are common things in our society. I've been raised by my mom, who completely dedicated her life to me. After graduating from school, I decided to go to the pedagogical university in Poltava and become an English teacher. English was my favourite subject at school, and I was quite good at it. The decision to study foreign languages, including German, has indeed changed my life. It is due to this decision that I met my husband and moved to another country. Of course, it would happen much later, but when I was still a student, my dream was to finish my studies and to find a nice job. Kyiv, the capital of Ukraine, was my dream destination. There are plenty of international organizations, language schools, hotels, banks and other institutions there where I could find my place in the sun and accomplish my career goals. Looking back at the four years of university, I can say that those years were the best in my life up until then, and the entire world lay wide open in front of me.

Coming from a family with a modest income, I started to look for a little job in my second year of studying. In Ukraine, as in the other post-Soviet countries, foreign languages are valued, and you can always make some pocket money giving private lessons or carrying out some translation tasks. The students who spoke English well enough could work part-time as interpreters in a translation bureau, travel agency or marriage agency, which were very popular at that time. They are still popular now, I believe. One of my university friends worked there, and I also decided to try this field. My responsibilities at the marriage agency were to translate letters written by Ukrainian men and women to people abroad and then to translate the responses. The pay for a student was quite decent, and I happily grabbed the opportunity to work there. Besides, it was a brilliant chance to practice my English, as, at that time, I could not afford to go to any English-speaking countries. To work with foreigners is to kill two birds with one stone, one might say. Finding an American or any foreign boyfriend and leaving Ukraine were never my goals. I was very attached to my country and my family. Even if I was poor, as it might appear in the eyes of a European citizen, I was happy in my surroundings and in my motherland.

I spent almost two years working at that place before I met my future husband. I think it would be unnecessary to tell his story, but one detail should be mentioned: When he came to Ukraine, he was young (twenty-nine years old), unmarried, adventurous and very romantic. Moreover, he was determined to create a family with a woman from Ukraine, as we were, according to him, perceived abroad as very family-oriented. He wrote a letter to the agency a few days before his arrival and asked for an interpreter to help him see the city and meet people. I was assigned to be his interpreter, and we had to spend a weekend together. Here, the story takes a romantic turn. We spent two days together, walking around Poltava, visiting Orthodox churches and eating Ukrainian food, which was so bizarre for my foreign friend. When it was the time to say goodbye to each other, my husband asked me if I would like to keep in touch and maybe to meet again. I agreed, and he started to come to see me every month, for almost a year. After that, he proposed and we got married. My mom did not try to prevent our marriage, even though she realized that I would live very far from her and would not be able to see her as often as before. She shared my happiness and encouraged me in all ways when I had some difficulties abroad.

After

The process of organizing all the necessary documents and getting a visa was quite long-winded and complicated. It took me about six months to arrange the papers, and I had to go to the Swiss Embassy in Kyiv many times. I was eager to be with my husband, so I made all possible efforts to make it happen. My feelings of happiness and love were mixed with anxiety and sadness over leaving my family and my country. That made me quite a sentimental person and changed my mood constantly. I remember well the day when I had my flight to Geneva, Switzerland. I remember the huge bag I packed with my mom's help. The bag seemed to be impossible to shift. I remember my last dinner at home and a long trip to the airport in nasty weather. But, most of all, I remember as if it were yesterday the sad smile on my mom's face. We both knew that our lives would never be the same again.

My bitter thoughts completely disappeared when I arrived in my new domicile. My husband tried to make it as comfortable as possible, to make me feel at home. The first months, we travelled a lot, to all corners of Switzerland. That was a great start for me. Already, in the first months of my living in a new country, I had quite a clear picture of its peculiarities, traditions and places of interest. To learn a new language, namely French, was a real challenge for me. Being completely in love with English, I forced myself to produce sounds and build constructions which, in my eyes, were very strange and illogical. Such a careless and, at times, disdainful attitude toward French was absolutely unreasonable and caused me many problems in the future. Now I can say with certainty that the local language is an inseparable part of the country you are living in, and the better your command of it, the better your integration into the society.

The first months in Switzerland were very quiet and even boring for me, since I did not know many people, and my circle of my friends was limited to those of my husband. I mostly stayed at home, studied some French and chatted with my family and friends on Skype. One might say that my body left Ukraine but not my soul. I still read Ukrainian newspapers and journals, worried about social events and demonstrated a keen interest in Ukrainian life. Nevertheless, as every young person who wants to be occupied and progress does, I decided to find a little job in order to meet people and study the language. After a few weeks of searching, I was hired in a small bar to work as a barmaid. Fortunately, a Russian girl worked there, and we easily found much in common. After this acquaintance, my social life improved because she introduced me to other Russian-speaking people, who formed a small community in Neuchâtel.

Six months after my arrival, I began courses at the University of Neuchâtel to continue my studies. In the beginning, it was very difficult for me because the system of education is extremely different to the Ukrainian one. Thus, I became a student for the next three years. The Russian girl I worked with had also started at this university, and we tried to manage all the difficulties together. Besides, my command of French noticeably improved, and I was already able to extend the circle of my friends. I started to communicate with other students, Swiss and foreign. That gave me a sense of being a part of something bigger than my previous life in Switzerland, at home in front of the computer. In the course of my studies, I met many nice people with whom I still keep in touch. Of course, I should admit that most of my friends are Ukrainian- or Russian-speaking and just a few have other nationalities. The language barrier, as well as the cultural one, the mentality, plays a central role when meeting people and trying to establish connections. It does not necessarily mean that local people are hostile to foreigners or to immigrants from ex-Soviet countries in particular. Rather, it is occasional misunderstandings and misinterpretation of some intentions and behaviour that create a gap in our communication. From my personal experience, I can say that this gap becomes smaller and smaller as you integrate into the society you are living in.

After six years living abroad, I can note a few difficulties and perhaps give a little advice. There are different reasons why people immigrate. Woman emigrants are a common phenomenon in Ukraine. There is a huge Ukrainian community in Italy, Canada, Poland and many other countries, a considerable part of which are women. Some of them are married to foreigners; some are working in order to get more money for their families in Ukraine. Some are looking for work, others for family, but all of them are searching for a better life. The reason for my immigration is marriage and the creation of a family. From my point of view, this is the best reason to immigrate and the easiest way to integrate into a foreign society. When you have a loving person by your side who can hold you every time you fall or give up, because the adopted country is a new battlefield, and who can also support you financially, your integration is much quicker, smoother and more pleasant. I know some girls who came to Switzerland for money. Some are working here, and a few are married to quite rich men. All these girls share the same bitter experience: Their lives are incomplete and even meaningless to some extent, either because they are unsatisfied with their jobs and have to carry out this everyday routine or because they do not love their husbands and live like birds in golden cages. All of them are still very attached to their native countries and, in a sense, lost in between.

I will always remember one woman whom I met at the Swiss Embassy when arranging papers for my visa. She told me that she had already been living in Switzerland for almost twenty years but she still came to Ukraine a few times a year to see her family. She said that after all these years abroad, she always felt frustrated, as if she were stuck in between the countries and cultures. She lost close ties with the Ukrainian reality but never established new ones in Switzerland. At that time, I did not really understand her feelings, and I thought that they were due to her personal failure to integrate in the new country. I still think that was, indeed, a part of the problem. But after all these years abroad, I've begun to understand that woman better, since I have met with some of the same difficulties myself. Sometimes, no matter how good my French is, the destructive questions about my lovely accent and peculiar Slavic appearance undermine all my efforts to look like an ordinary Swiss citizen. Of course, my new homeland is very multinational and multilingual, and the accent is not a surprise for the locals. Yet this question hunts me incessantly, no matter what I do or where I go, and it forces me to constantly keep in mind that I am an outsider, a stranger. I always answer politely that I am from Ukraine, though I have already forgotten what it was actually like to be Ukrainian. The feeling that you do not belong to the society you are living in slows down your integration.

Another difficulty with immigration is achieving your professional goals and building a career in the field you are interested in. From my personal experience, I know that some professions which were considered prestigious in Ukraine are regarded as less profitable in Switzerland. Some diplomas, too, cannot be validated in this country and demand further education. In Ukraine, I could work as a teacher at a school due to my pedagogical education, but in Switzerland, I have to start from scratch and go again to a local pedagogical school. On the one hand, it is completely logical that the Swiss job market is different and has its peculiarities. Hence, coming from another part of the world, you need to adjust to it and meet the employers' requirements. On the other hand, if you are a newcomer, it could take you quite a lot of time to first learn how the system works and then adapt to it. In my case, it took me almost five years to get certain insights into it. That significantly slowed down my professional development.

From my point of view, and it is of course a subjective opinion, Switzerland is a country ruled by men, and for women it is sometimes quite hard to break through this shield. One of my Russian girl-friends was asked at a job interview, "Why do you want to work if you are married? Wouldn't you rather be thinking of having kids?" She was absolutely disappointed in, and even angry at, such a question, and, consequently, her professional search bore no fruits. This example is perhaps not representative, but this type of situation is still all too often present. I think that many woman immigrants hear such remarks, if not personally then indirectly. What happened a few times to me is rather a reproach that I come from a Third World country and that I am incompetent in the Swiss job market. My pedagogical education is also irrelevant, since Ukraine is not in the European Union. Yet, I can agree only in part. I believe that, overall, children are the same everywhere across the world, and, first and foremost, they need love and care. These kinds of reproaches or comments automatically put me in the inferior position in relation to my interlocutor.

Some Swiss went even further in their misunderstanding of my native country. They asked me if I visited school in Ukraine and whether the school was located in the open air, somewhere in the backwoods. I am always confused by such questions and cannot find a decent answer at once. As a matter of fact, the superior attitude, misinterpretation, misunderstanding and unfair judgments are factors which make you feel very uncomfortable and sometimes even horrible in your alleged new homeland. Consequently, you start to think that probably there is indeed something wrong with you and you are not good enough for this country. As a result, you have low self-esteem and you cannot overcome the feeling of inferiority that grows very fast in you every time you encounter such people. If it could be some relief for women who have the same experience, I would advise not taking it too much to heart and instead considering these people themselves incompetent. I think that this type of remark can be found in every country, no matter where you go. Maybe just in your native country the perception of them would be different. When we are far from our home, we take these remarks at face value and believe in them because of lack of experience or knowledge. Now, when I'm asked such questions, I advise these people to make better acquaintance with Ukraine and probably get more information about it. The lack of knowledge does not allow them to draw premature conclusions.

These are the major problems I encountered when I changed country. Certainly, there is a considerable list of difficulties and advantages to moving to another country I have not mentioned. I do not want to dissuade or encourage somebody to take this or that decision. Rather, the idea I try to convey here is that life is full of pleasant and bitter surprises, regardless of the country you live in. It is true that in Ukraine these surprises were different to the ones in Switzerland, but in general we can escape or avoid neither one nor the other. On the contrary, we need to be strong enough to deal with them in any country and in any circumstances. What I would advise is to be sincere in your desires and motives. Build your future life abroad on a solid, even if unprofitable, background, rather than searching for easy money or a "golden cage." In the latter case, your life could turn into something very tragic. I do not suggest abandoning the idea of finding a good job abroad or marrying a kind-hearted man. If this feeling is true and your heart is pure, then you will easily integrate into the foreign society and fully develop your skills and talents. In this case, your life could be an adventure and a beautiful journey worthy of a novel. But if your motives to leave your country are limited to easy money, scamming and idle life, I would not advise you to give in to the temptations, because things could turn out completely different in a new country. Hard work, patience and commitment to your goals will help you to find a new home and be happy wherever you go. I can say for sure that I have two homes now which makes me very happy. Ukraine remains my motherland, the country of my birth and the place where my family lives. It is always in my heart and in my soul. Yet Switzerland has also found its own place in my heart, and I love it as much as Ukraine. My wish for everybody is to find yourself, to find your life path and to open your heart to the country you are living in.

Ann Croucher

Courage

My grandmother, Jessie Lavinia Burrows, was born into poverty in London's East End in 1889. They lived a stone's throw away from Tobacco Dock and the River Thames. Her parents, Emily and William Burrows, were unskilled and largely uneducated and struggled to survive in the harsh conditions of the time.

Jessie's father stayed with the family long enough to have six children, although two died in early infancy. Similarly to many other slum-dwellers at the time, he spent much of his time drinking because alcohol was a cheap way to escape life. Emily eventually tired of his behaviour. Following a particularly violent row, she took his dinner to the pub and dumped it on his head. He left, and as far as the children knew, he was never seen again.

Despite his failings as a parent, his presence had at least ensured a roof over their heads. His desertion plunged the family into destitution. This was a time when women were allowed to own nothing. They were unable to sign rental agreements or even to work once they married. Jessie recounted freezing nights spent huddled in shop doorways with the younger children while her mother drank in the pubs. Bill, her little brother, worked for a costermonger, the East Enders' name for a market trader. The costers used to leave unsold fruit and vegetables out on their market stalls for the poor to take at the end of the day, and sometimes Bill managed to get the children a hot potato to eat.

London at this time was in the throes of a mini ice age. The Thames froze over more than once, and with money, food and fuel in short supply, the children were sent barefoot to the muddy edges of the river to scavenge discarded food, wood and embers. Nowadays, these "mudlarks," as they were called, have a slightly romantic reputation—finding pieces of pottery, coins and fossils from an earlier time—but as far as Jessie and her family were concerned, foraging in the sewer that was the Thames meant survival. She was usually cold and nearly always hungry. She never grew above five feet tall because of malnutrition.

Inevitably, the time came when they began a series of stays in workhouses. Inhumane and brutal as these places were, they meant that the children survived. Jessie told me of a time she and her sister Lizzie were set to work scrubbing a flagstone corridor with cold water and scrubbing brushes, on their knees. Jessie was eight and Lizzie was six. Just as they finished cleaning the long corridor, one of the adults in charge walked up it with muddy boots, kicked over the bucket and told them to do it again. Their mother, Emily, was put into the Ratcliffe workhouse in Shadwell, situated on the infamous Ratcliffe highway and known for its thieves, pickpockets and brothels.

When Jessie was eleven, she was sent to a "school" in Surrey. It was another workhouse which trained the girls for "service." This service was menial work where the girls obtained a position in houses with better-off families, cleaning, setting fires, emptying chamber pots. Pay was usually just bed and board, and the working hours were unbearably long. Later in life, Jessie could never look at pickled beetroot because she was so very hungry one day that she ate an entire stone jar of it and was sick for hours. She spoke very fondly of the Jewish families who had employed her because they were kind. There she was well fed and treated kindly, clothed properly and kept warm. Many of the other families she worked for treated her more like a slave.

The family rebounded in and out of the workhouse for years. One of Jessie's brothers, Bill, joined the Royal Navy. It was a common way to escape poverty at that time, but he died at nineteen when, during World War One, his ship, *Irresistible*, was torpedoed in the Dardanelles.

Jessie married and, in late 1909, had a baby girl named Isabel. It was at this stage that her life became, if it was possible, even harder. Family lore says that her husband was "difficult," a lot older than her and violent. From this, it isn't difficult to see why Jessie ended up, in 1911, at the age of twenty-one, on a ship to New Zealand with her very young baby. The events leading to this were only known to her, but it seems very likely that she just ran, and her husband was unlikely to track her to New Zealand. She was apparently sponsored by "the Duke of Norfolk's Catholic Resettlement Agency."

Jessie spoke little about her time as a steerage passenger. She described being below deck for the whole journey and suffering from debilitating seasickness, sleeping between cargo boxes, and some of the sailors smuggling extra rations down to her and her baby. The journey took months because the ship was making deliveries; it wasn't a passenger vessel.

She arrived eventually and found work as a cook at a logging camp in Taumarunui, in the North Island. The settlement was remote and harsh, and the loggers were hard men. She lived in a tent for two years in a climate which wasn't best suited to outdoor living.

As Jessie came from a generation which kept their own counsel, the next part of the story has been pieced together from other people's accounts, rather than from hers. My grandfather, Sydney Good, always said that he got a working passage and then jumped ship in New Zealand to be with my grandmother. He came from Stanmore, Middlesex, UK. Whatever the reason, and whatever the paternity of Isabel (Bella), her death at sixteen months from pneumonia is registered under Syd's surname in Taumarunui, and her grave is probably lost in the bush surrounding the area at the time. There is little doubt that the conditions she endured in her short life had much to do with her death, but lack of medical facilities and a thirty-mile horseback ride to the nearest large town didn't do much to improve the situation.

Having settled and made a home, Jessie sponsored her mother and two siblings to join her in New Zealand, where they remained and had their own families.

Eventually, Syd and Jessie were awarded a piece of land, and Syd built their house from trees he logged in the bush. The land wasn't particularly productive, and Syd found work as a bridge and viaduct builder as this "new" country began to take shape. Jessie was left to run the farm, taking the long trip to the nearest town every six months for supplies. She managed to feed her growing family with their own produce and livestock. She often spoke of the chickens running indoors for scraps and the cow poking its head through the window, shouting to be milked. Though it wasn't easy, she spoke fondly of her life in New Zealand.

There was no running water or electricity, so medical treatment was primitive. Jessie became adept at sewing up cuts and treating ailments with plants from the bush, guided by the Māori, who did all they could to help. She told of one Māori chief who came to their home loaded with gifts of rugs, cloaks and livestock, asking her to join his tribe and be his wife. For years, there was a Māori cloak made of kiwi feathers hidden in an old trunk in her house, which she said was to be her wedding cloak.

Jessie's second baby died aged four from peritonitis caused by appendicitis, despite having been taken by cart to the nearest hospital. It was an eight-hour trip away. It was too late, and the little girl, Alice, was buried in a cemetery in Hamilton, where the hospital was situated.

Jessie went on to have a boy and three girls in this remote place, twenty miles from the next farm and habitation. While she was pregnant with one of the children, she was kicked in the stomach by a cow, and her baby was born with some facial damage. Though the life was hard in New Zealand, they had made money, and things were much easier than they had been in her early childhood.

In 1927, Jessie took her daughter to London for facial surgery, along with her youngest child, who was just seven. She left her two eldest children in charge of the farm. Her son was about nineteen and her daughter twenty-one. The trip was a lengthy one: three months out, two months for surgery and recovery, and three months to get home again. Her son was always a bit wild, and it seems that Jessie's time away became a chance for him and his sister to party with their friends. In any event, when Jessie returned, she found her daughter was pregnant. She was sent away to have the baby, and when she returned, the child was registered as Jessie and Syd's daughter, rather than grandchild. The baby girl became part of the family, as was so common in families at this time. The truth of her birth was hidden from her until she was informed about the truth by a member of Jessie's sister's family, by which time both her mother and Jessie were dead.

It seems that Jessie felt this remote life was no good for her girls, and she returned to London in 1932, leaving her son and his father to sell the farm and join them later. Her son never came to London, though Syd left him to finish up the sale of the farm and came "home" to his family. Their son never sent money from the sale of the farm back to his family and ended up bankrupt. Naturally, this left Jessie and her girls without an income, although they had bought a house. They were reduced once more to going to the markets when they closed for the unsold fruit and vegetables.

She did leave her sisters and their families behind in New Zealand, and she missed them terribly. Communication has changed so much in the last century. Syd worked outside the home and returned to New Zealand once or twice to try to sell the farm. Ever resourceful, Jessie opened a theatrical boarding house, since they lived very near a music hall. They had such names as Johnny Weissmuller and Benny Hill staying there when they were performing at the music hall and theatre in Brixton.

The 1930s weren't the best time to be returning to London. The Great Depression was followed by World War Two in 1939, and though Jessie always intended to return to New Zealand, she never made it back. She threw herself back into life as a Cockney, attending the music hall and joining many other families on the yearly trip to Kent as a hop-picker (effectively a paid holiday). On these trips, they stayed in the corrugated iron sheds, slept on straw mattresses, and sat around fires singing and chatting at night.

In 1962, Syd died from the flu, and Jessie sold up her house in London and left to live near one of her girls in Suffolk. Syd was the love of her life, and she never really recovered from his loss. She spoke of him constantly and said she'd soon be with him.

She died in 1974, having lived a life that was harder and richer than any of us could imagine. New Zealand promised a new and better life, and, in many ways, that is what it gave her. Jessie wrote to her sisters as frequently as the communications of the time would allow, but she never went back and never again saw her mother or her siblings. She talked about them and their lives, reliving their good and bad times both in London and in New Zealand. She talked about the sense of isolation and vulnerability living so far away from medical help, and about her grief for the loss of her two babies. I was young when she spoke about these things, but her stories have stayed with me. The courage that made a very young woman take her baby alone to a country that she didn't know and build a new life has marked me. My mother, her daughter, always wanted to return to the time when she ran wild in the Kiwi bush, but she never went back in her lifetime. After her death, our British and New Zealand families came together to scatter her ashes in the place she loved.

Kay Ross

Finding Joy in Change

I have lived in Canada for most of my life now. My sister and I left Guyana at the same time. We were born and grew up in Guyana. I went to Prince Edward Island (PEI) to attend university, and my sister went to university in Montreal, Quebec, also in Canada.

Guyana is a small country and is the only English-speaking country in South America. Therefore, Guyanese identify more with the islands in the Caribbean, especially if English is their native tongue. PEI is the smallest province in Canada, and there are many similarities between the two places. Guyana and Canada are both members of the British Commonwealth. English is the official language of Guyana, and English and French are the official languages of Canada. PEI appealed to me because of its small size. The acceptance letters from the university and the residence were very personal. I was advised not to worry about buying warm clothing. I was assured that someone would take me shopping when I arrived there. A welcoming letter from a Guyanese student who was enrolled in Pre-Engineering was also included. I was sold.

My sister and I travelled together to Montreal, and then I went on to PEI. We had no idea that Canada was such a huge country. We had planned to get together on the weekends. I missed one of my connections and had to overnight in New Brunswick. I realized then that seeing each other on weekends would not be possible, as the train took a full day.

We considered ourselves to be embarking on an adventure. We tried to imagine what it would be like to be cold. In preparation, we put our hands inside the freezer and left them there for a short time. Nothing in Guyana could have prepared me for winter. I was freezing when I arrived in September and didn't think it could possibly become much colder. Against all good advice, I donned my winter coat—an action that I came to regret, as I should have saved it for when I really needed it. However, I remember being in class and looking out the window at the first snowflakes of the season. It was magical, and I was mesmerised.

The university was originally a Catholic one, but it is now a provincial institution. It was a Catholic university for the first of my four years there. The residence was run by the kindest nuns imaginable. My first morning in residence, I awoke to loud banging and clanking. I thought to myself, work certainly starts early here. I asked one of the gentle nuns if there was work being done outside my bedroom window. Seeing the puzzled look on her face, I escorted her to my room to hear the noise for herself. She explained that it was an old building and that noise was the furnace starting up. Coming from a tropical climate, I had never seen or heard of such a thing.

My sister and I spent our first Canadian Christmas together in Montreal. During that holiday season, I was surprised to see children playing in the snow. I couldn't believe my eyes when, hours later, the same children were still outside. I couldn't understand why parents would allow their children out in such extreme temperatures. I soon learned that adults as well as children regularly took part in outdoor activities during all four seasons of the year.

The main industries in PEI are farming and fishing. PEI is famous for its potatoes. And lobsters and other seafood are shipped worldwide. It is a well-known tourist destination, too. As with many small communities, there is a slower pace and the residents are known for being friendly.

I had planned on returning to Guyana when I finished my studies. I had been looking forward to never wearing winter clothing on a regular basis. In fact, I had already promised to give most of the items away. But I met my husband at university, and he had lived in PEI all his life. We decided to remain there, where we worked and raised our two children. My son, after living overseas, has returned to PEI. After my husband passed away, I moved to Nova Scotia, where I live with my daughter and her family.

While at university, I became close friends with the other foreign students. My roommate was from Hong Kong, and we have maintained close contact over the years. During the various holidays, most of the foreign students remained on campus because it was too expensive to go home. We entertained ourselves, and it helped us not to be overcome with homesickness. Sharing stories about our families and homeland was also therapeutic. Many students were interested in hearing about our culture, customs and food. I learned that children all over the world have the same interests when growing up.

When I moved out of the university community, I found myself seeking Guyanese and others from the Caribbean who also lived in PEI. In time, I found similar friendships to the ones I had formed at university. We would look forward to getting together at least a couple of times a year. We shared meals from our homeland and listened to the music of our youth. Our families enjoyed these events as much as we did, especially our children.

My husband and children have been to Guyana with me on a few occasions. I was pleased that they had the opportunity to learn more about my childhood. My sister lives in the house where I grew up, so we were fortunate to be able to stay there. The headmistress of my high school took us on a tour of my old school, pointing out the changes. We visited relatives, friends and neighbours. Although my children grew up in PEI, they immediately felt an affinity for Guyana. They had only known their Canadian cousins until then, and now they felt complete. I am acutely aware of the better standard of living my family and I have had in Canada, but I'll never forget my carefree childhood. I especially think of Guyana during the winter. I remember the palm trees, the different smells, sights and sounds of day and night. Then, here in Canada, spring comes alive: I see the buds on the trees, I feel the warmth of the sun, and there is a fresh smell in the air. I enthusiastically dream of summer days barbequing, going to the beach and generally appreciating my life. Realizing that even when fall comes around I will find joy in the changing leaves makes it all worthwhile.

My life in PEI has been both challenging and rewarding. Canada's smallest province lacked diversity when I lived there. Most residents were of Irish, Scottish or French descent. My mother-in-law was Irish, and my father-in-law was Scottish. I am mainly of African descent. There were few visible minorities and even fewer inter-racial couples. I became accustomed to being stared at. In fact, I could understand why, because I was surprised when I met someone from another country, too. I wholeheartedly embraced the Irish and Scottish culture, music and food. I also introduced my newly acquired relatives to my culture, music and food, which they thoroughly enjoyed. I worked for the provincial government and was a voting delegate for my union. At the school my children attended, I chaired a committee for the Home and School Association. I was involved in the Catholic Women's League at my church, including positions as Secretary and President. This enabled me to meet like-minded people and form lasting friendships. I enjoyed visiting relatives and friends in Toronto, Ontario, Canada. Toronto has a large Guyanese and Caribbean population, and there are many occasions for celebrations. The Toronto Caribbean Carnival, Caribana, attracts expatriates from far and wide.

Since moving to Halifax, Nova Scotia, I have enjoyed being around the different nationalities that I so missed in PEI. As luck would have it, my next-door neighbour is also Guyanese. She has lived in Halifax for most of her life and has immersed herself in the Guyanese and Caribbean community here. Through her, I was able to integrate into these communities, and this has given me great satisfaction and contentment. In addition, her husband is from Ghana, Africa. Therefore, I have been fortunate to become familiar with some African cultures as well.

I am retired but volunteer my services at my church here in Halifax. I am also a member of a West Indian Commonwealth Society. Nova Scotia, being a slightly larger province, lends itself to more opportunities to be involved in community activities. I have the time to teach my grandchildren about their heritage and to be proud of their roots. I want them to learn about and respect the different cultures that they encounter on a daily basis.

For those immigrants with no ties to their new country, there are many organizations willing to lend a helping hand. There are volunteers to assist if they have language difficulties or need help finding employment and generally obtaining the necessities to feel at home. There are families, church groups and other committees willing and ready to offer support and friendship if need be. As Canada is mainly populated by immigrants, many Canadians have shared the same experiences. Those who immigrate from the same country usually form their own groups and welcome new members with open arms.

As I reflect on the changes over my lifetime, I notice much more diversity when I visit PEI. In fact, the whole face of Canada is changing. I am optimistic that immigrants will have a good life here. When I was a student, even a telephone call home was a major investment. Needless to say, travel was out of reach. Now, with advanced technology, maintaining contact with family and friends is easy and convenient and can even be free. My hope is for all immigrants to be welcomed and valued in their new country.

Sara Sheffield-Cavallo

The Language of Love

I was, for the most part, comfortable in my old life. I was brought up in a well-off middle-class American family. I was always interested in and open to other cultures growing up, partly due to the fact that my parents were in the military and had travelled and lived overseas frequently when I was very young. My brother was even born at Incirlik Air Base in Turkey, and some of my earliest memories are of when we lived in Wiesbaden, Germany. Despite this, I had never imagined myself choosing to immigrate to another country. Why would I? The USA was my home, and I was comfortable there.

The idea of immigration started when I was a freshman in college. It was there that I met Darry. We met in a speech class. It was the only speech class that I was required to take for my major, which was Nursing. The first day of class, our professor had us all tell the class where we were from. Darry said that he was Italian and French. He was an international student. I didn't think much about it at the time, but a good friend who was also in the speech class noticed the Italian student right away. We decided to ask him to go to lunch with us and some of our friends. He accepted, and that's how we got to know each other. After some weeks had gone by, a few of my friends brought to my attention the fact that Darry seemed interested in me as more than just a friend. I said that I didn't want to get too interested in him because the thought of dating someone who wasn't an American seemed too complicated. Little did I know that I would end up marrying him!

Darry and I dated all through our college years, and things were getting pretty serious near the end of our senior year. Despite my hopes, Darry was not at all interested in immigrating to the United States. He had his own goals and plans, which he wanted to accomplish in Europe. After graduation, we both went our separate ways. I needed to gain experience in my field as a Registered Nurse, and Darry wanted to secure work in France, which is where his family lived at the time. It was a difficult road ahead, but we managed to maintain a long-distance relationship. The economic situation in France was less than ideal, and Darry did not find a stable place of employment there. After a year and a half of searching, Darry found employment in Switzerland, thanks to some acquaintances of his family.

Things were finally falling into place. Even though I adored my family and felt accomplished with the work that I had as a labour and delivery nurse, I knew that I loved Darry and that I wanted to be with him and start our own family together someday. Darry and I talked often of marriage, and we had both agreed that it would be best if Darry secured employment before this happened. When Darry was hired in Switzerland, the opportunity for our marriage finally arrived. Darry and I married, and so my immigration to Switzerland had started. It was a place that I knew very little of at the time, but I went there motivated by love, the love that I had for my new husband. We didn't have much when I came to Switzerland, just like most couples when they are first married. Darry had been renting a bedroom with an en suite bathroom from a nice middle-aged couple who owned a townhouse. He had briefly looked into renting a few apartments but with no success. Affordable housing can be quite hard to find in Switzerland, since the cost of living there is one of the highest in the world. We lived together for the first two months as a married couple in that rented room.

I didn't have a job lined up when I came to Switzerland. I didn't even speak the language. Darry would go to work Monday through

Friday from 8 AM to 6 PM. I stayed in our rented room for a good part of the day, trying to learn French through language-learning computer software. I was barely able to communicate with the couple who rented us the room. We used a mixture of English, French and non-verbal language cues. At times, this led to frustration for both parties. Things started to look up after a month of being there. I was offered a job interview at a local day care through the daughter-in-law of the couple that we were living with. The director of the day care spoke English, so that assuaged my fears of not being able to express myself. The interview went well. I was offered a limited contract of six months as an intern. The job was very poorly paid, since it was designed for students who worked there as part of their practical training, but it was definitely better than nothing, and I would be immersed in French at the same time.

My work at the day care was difficult at times, but it was necessary for my immersion in the language and culture of the land. Like with any job anywhere, there were nice and not-so-nice co-workers. The nice ones made attempts at speaking with me even if their English was not very good. I could tell that they felt sorry for me because they knew that I was working there just to learn French and that it must have been difficult for me to not be able to express myself well. Some of the other, less kind, co-workers seemed to view my working at the day care as a nuisance more than anything else. One of the educators complained about me to the director, saying that I wasn't able to discipline the rowdy children well enough and that I lacked motivation. I felt betrayed, like this person was taking advantage of me. I thought to myself that I would like to see this person come to the United States and try to discipline children without knowing how to speak English! I was always appreciated at my old jobs, so this experience was new for me.

During this time, I had begun to experience Swiss culture in my day-to-day life. I took French evening classes once per week for a few months, and this helped improve my French immensely. It was also fun meeting other foreigners who were adjusting to the language and culture. The Swiss food was very good—especially if, like me, you are into good cheese and chocolate. Apart from the famous dishes of cheese fondue and raclette (melted cheese on potatoes), the local specialties include sausage stuffed with cabbage and buttered perch fillets sourced directly from the Swiss lakes. The town that we lived in was settled along a large lake, and there were many nice walking trails and sandy beaches. I could tell right away that the Swiss pride themselves on being very natural. They put a heavy emphasis on conservation. This included the recycling of everything: aluminium cans, plastic bottles, glass, batteries, paper, cardboard and compost. They even have special trash bags that you are required to use. These trash bags are very costly, at 1.95 Swiss francs per medium-sized bag, to keep everyone motivated to recycle. The grocery stores in Switzerland were quite small compared to the grocery stores in the USA and in France. We sometimes drove to France, which was forty minutes away from where we lived, to have a larger selection of goods at a more affordable price than in Switzerland. The hours of operation for the stores in Switzerland were something that we had to adjust to, as well. Most of the stores closed their doors by 6:30 PM during the week, 4:30 PM on Saturdays, and were completely closed on Sundays. Swiss people told us that things were like this so that the store workers could have a decent home/work life balance. The Swiss people that we had met so far were polite yet reserved. Since we had no family or friends in our new country of residence, we tried to be as social as possible. We started attending a church in our town, and we tried to get to know our work colleagues.

A few weeks passed by, I was somehow able to convince my critics at the day care that I was doing a better job, and my six-month contract was renewed for a second time, allowing me to stay employed there for a full year. I made progress in French during that year at the day care, and I was happy about this accomplishment. I still had a long way to go before my level of French was considered good enough for the Swiss Red Cross. This is the organization that accepts or denies foreign-earned nursing degrees. Fear and stress were starting to sink in. I would soon be unemployed, and we needed another salary in order to continue to pay the rent on our new apartment, as well as all of our other monthly bills. With the help of my husband, who speaks French fluently, I started applying online for nursing jobs at different clinics. To my amazement, one of the clinics replied to me within a week or two of my application. I received a phone call from the general director of the clinic, and she scheduled me for an interview the next week.

The clinic was about an hour away from where I lived, in a town called Montreux. Although this would be a far commute for me, it was in an unbelievably beautiful setting on the Lake Geneva shoreline, with the Swiss and French Alps on the other side of the lake. This area is referred to as the Swiss Riviera. I think it is one of the most beautiful in Switzerland and possibly even the world.

It was clear after living a year in Switzerland that this was a wealthy country. How could this be the case for such a small country with few exported natural resources? One of the reasons is the world-renowned Swiss banks that offer rich clients their "banking secret," creating a sort of fiscal paradise for them. This was especially seen in Montreux. Designer stores and luxury hotels lined the main street, catering to wealthy tourists and residents alike.

I was interviewed by the head doctor of the clinic. He was a tall, serious, middle-aged man from Iran. At first, we spoke in French, but we switched to speaking in English. He could see that I still had some learning to do. He reassured me, though, that many of the employees and clients of the clinic spoke English and that was why my CV stood out to him. He explained to me that the clinic was in a hotel that operated both with and apart from the clinic. Most of the clients who came to the clinic were wealthy people from China, Russia and the Middle East, and other parts of Europe and the Americas. Since the clinic was private, I would be able to be hired as a medical assistant/nurse even though my American nursing degree had not been recognized by the Swiss Red Cross. I was asked, however, during my interview, to continue my attempts to obtain the Swiss recognition. I was hired that day, and I accepted the position with enthusiasm. This truly was a miracle for me! I had been hired in my field of work, in a foreign country whose language was different from my own, at the exact moment when I needed a huge pay increase. I felt God's provision and presence in my life more than ever before.

My early days at the clinic were a bit of a challenge. At first, I thought that I would be working mostly with the nursing team, but that was not the case. The primary position that needed filling was that of a medical assistant, which is a different role than that of a nurse. Medical assistants perform a lot of office administration tasks, such as transcribing medical reports, organizing medical appointments, medical coding, and filing medical reports. I wasn't going to let this rattle me. I needed this job. One of my co-workers was pretty vocal about not being very convinced that I would be an asset to the team. She focused on my flaws of not being able to speak French well and on the fact that I didn't even have a medical-assistant diploma. She and others at the clinic asked me if I personally knew or had ties to someone in administration. They thought that this would have been the only likely reason why someone like me was hired to work there. It took a couple of weeks for me to adapt to this new line of work, but I was determined not to let this criticism sway my resolve. I continued to do my work as best I could, and as time went by, I was able to earn the respect of my co-workers.

I grew to enjoy my work at the clinic, and I made good friends there. Most of the clients and employees at this clinic were foreigners or immigrants themselves, and that really helped me feel at ease. I was able to understand their struggles of living in a country that was not their own because their struggles were the same as mine: missing family members, language barriers, diploma recognition problems . . . we had a lot in common. I had also made friends with my Swiss co-workers. This gave me more insight into their culture and ways of thinking. I was also able to understand some of their concerns and mentalities regarding over-immigration and wanting to protect their own economy and identity in the world.

During my many talks with my Swiss co-workers, I realized that certain immigrant groups coming from countries with very different cultural backgrounds than Switzerland were sometimes not seen in a good light. These immigrants were viewed as stealing jobs or benefits from the Swiss and infiltrating traditional Swiss culture with a culture that was different from their own. The Swiss are known for being good workers and superior craftspeople, producing quality products such as luxury handcrafted watches. When large groups of people come into the country and disrespect these traditions, it is understandably not appreciated.

During my time working at the clinic, I continued my quest to become recognized as a nurse in Switzerland. I felt like this was necessary in order to really be able to settle long-term here. Even though Darry worked a full-time job that he was passionate about, he was underpaid for Swiss living standards. I knew that I would have to do my part financially, and becoming recognized would mean a higher salary as well as job security. My husband and I enjoy being able to eat out and go shopping from time to time. We also love travelling and going on vacations. We were able to visit various cities in Italy, France, Germany, Ireland, Canada, England, Spain and the Czech Republic while living in Switzerland. If I hadn't been able to work, we would never have been able to afford these trips. Just paying our regular monthly bills would have been a challenge. Up until now, we had been able to visit my family in the US every year during summer or Christmas vacations. This was a special time for me to be able to reconnect with my family, and I did not want to have to give that up due to poor finances.

The Red Cross communicated to me that I needed to accomplish three things for nursing recognition: first, to pass a standardized test proving that my French was a level B2; second, to take some additional classes that would cost 6,500 Swiss francs (roughly equivalent to US dollars); and, finally, to work six months full-time without pay as a nurse intern in a general hospital setting in Switzerland. I was willing to fulfil these arduous requirements, despite the obvious challenges it placed on me. I bought a self-study book specifically for the French test that I needed to pass. I applied for the test and took it after a few months of studying. The results came in: I had passed the test at the B2 level! One requirement down, two more to go! I applied for the nursing classes, which started only once per year. All had been going well, and it seemed that I would be accepted for the required nursing classes. One day, a few weeks before the start of the classes, I received a phone call from the school. A woman explained to me that I was missing a paper that proved that I spoke

French at the C1 level. I was dumbfounded. I hadn't realized that I would need to have this high level of French; after all, the Swiss Red Cross only required the B2 level. I explained this to the woman at the other end of the line, and she told me that it was a new requirement. The school found that students who had less than a C1 level in French did poorly in written exams. I didn't know what to think or say for a few seconds. I ended the conversation with the woman by saying that I would take the French test necessary to see if I had the C1 level. The day of the test came. I received the results the same day; my French level was intermediate B2 . . . not high enough for the nursing school. I was disappointed. I knew that I could not start the necessary classes for another year. I thought, *Why are the Red Cross and this school making it so hard for me to work as a nurse here?* Especially since there is a shortage of nurses in Switzerland, as in many places around the world.

At this point, I knew that, at least for now, obtaining my Swiss nursing recognition would not be possible. I had worked at the clinic in Montreux for two years when I decided that it was time for a change. The long commute time that I had to do every day of the week was wearing me down. I missed being able to just have time to relax and take care of things at our home. Also, we became really good friends with another married couple who lived in our town. He was Swiss, and she was American. They relocated to Switzerland after living for seven years in America together. We started doing things with them on a regular basis. We had a dog and they had two dogs, so we would do activities like hiking and letting the dogs run free in the fields. We also liked making bonfires in remote locations and barbequing food together. I had hobbies and interests other than work, but I wasn't able to focus on them as much as I wanted to because I was too tired. I decided to look for a job closer to home. This was not easy, since the hospitals and most of the publicly run healthcare institutions required foreign nurses to have the Swiss recognition. I eventually found a home health nurse job that was based in the town where I lived. Home health nursing is when nurses drive to the homes of their patients and perform various treatments in the home setting. This organization was privately owned, so I would be able to work as a nurse even without the Swiss recognition.

I interviewed with them and did a test day to see what the work would be like. I told them that I was looking for a job closer to home to cut down on my commute time. I was told that I would have a patient network in and around the town that I lived in and that I would not have to travel far. I accepted the position, ready for the change.

The first two days at my new job, I was paired with another nurse. After that, I was completely on my own. The types of care that I was expected to perform were quite advanced. The patients I visited were very sick and required highly technical nursing care. I saw this as a positive thing. I counted it as an opportunity to be doing "real" nursing. The downside, however, was that my commuting was even worse than before. I was required to visit people who lived in various areas that were forty-five minutes away or more. This was not what I had been told during my interview. Also, during the times in my schedule that I was supposed to have off, I was called constantly by the office asking me to help out with emergencies and see patients that weren't even mine. It became clear early on that this new job was not for me. I decided to resign.

This was not an easy decision. I had never left a job before without having something else in place. I think that the accumulation of various pressures was just too much. I felt overworked all of the time, but I didn't have much to show for it. We were both interested in owning a home of our own, but that seemed like an impossible dream due to the high home prices in Switzerland. We considered building a house on the property that Darry's parents owned in southern France, thinking that we could either move there or rent out the house as an investment. But legal constraints and finances hindered this project, so, for now, we put it aside. I knew that I would want to start a family in a few years, but I was apprehensive about doing this in Switzerland, since we didn't have any family there to help us. I felt in a way that it was partly the Swiss Red Cross's fault that I hadn't found a good place of employment, since they had made it so hard for me to become recognized as a nurse. Since I didn't have any other job lined up, I applied for Swiss unemployment. This was a new low in my life that I had never before experienced. I was embarrassed to have to use unemployment. It was something that I never wanted to use, but, given the circumstances, I didn't see any other way. Even though it was not an ideal situation, I still felt like God was providing for our needs.

I looked for and applied for many jobs during my time on unemployment. In order to continue to receive payments, I was required to apply for at least twelve jobs per month. A few people called me for interviews, but not having my Swiss nursing recognition was always an issue. Legally, places were not able to hire me as a nurse without it. I was assigned an unemployment caseworker and eventually placed in a local nursing home for a six-month contract. While it was not my ideal work setting, I was happy to be able to do something related to my field.

The head nurse of the nursing home took a quick liking to me and I to her. She was a thin middle-aged woman who was originally from Algeria but had grown up in France and studied nursing in Belgium. She wanted to hire me right away, but it was complicated, since I didn't have my Swiss recognition. This was brought to the attention of my unemployment case worker, who urged me to ask the Red Cross if they would be willing to recognize my American nursing degree as that of an ASSC (healthcare assistant) in Switzerland. Within a couple of weeks, I was officially recognized as an ASSC. The news was bittersweet. While an ASSC is a lesser title than that of a nurse, I was happy to at least have something that was recognized by Switzerland. The nursing home hired me immediately following this news.

I adapted quickly to my new job. I enjoyed the team that I worked with, which included a mix of Swiss people as well as many immigrants from countries such as Portugal, France, Morocco, Cameroon, Bosnia, Ukraine and Canada. The work was physically and emotionally hard at times, but, for the most part, our team worked through obstacles well together. I particularly enjoyed my talks with my boss, the head nurse. She and I agreed on a lot of things, such as the importance of a good work ethic and fighting hard for what you want and need in life. I understood that her life had not been a particularly easy one. She was an immigrant for economic and social reasons.

She had also undergone the change necessary to adjust to a different way of life.

The head nurse and the director of the nursing home encouraged me to continue my attempts at becoming recognized as a nurse in Switzerland. I was honest with my boss from the beginning in explaining that there was a chance that my husband and I could move back to the United States and that if this was the case, I wouldn't pursue the nursing recognition. She understood this. For a brief time, plans were in motion for me to continue on the pathway towards recognition, but these plans did not get very far. Darry and I attended a work conference in the US where the possibility of his being hired to work there was discussed. In a few months, we had started the immigration process for him to be able to move to the US with a green card. When he had lived in the US before, he was only there on a student visa.

I was thrilled at the idea of moving back to the US. For me, it was the answer to many difficulties that we faced in Switzerland. I was already a licensed Registered Nurse over there, so I would be able to further my education easily. Darry's bachelor's degree was American, so he should be able to further his education easily as well. The fact that my family lived there was reassuring, as we knew we would have help and company.

My husband didn't end up getting hired through the conference that we attended, but he had a desire to start a non-profit organization for different international ministries and charities. The US seemed like a good place to start this, since we had a lot of ministry-related contacts there. I started applying online for different nursing jobs. One of them contacted me pretty quickly for an interview. I made arrangements and flew from Switzerland to the US for the job interview. It went well, but they were looking to fill a position in less than two months. I explained my dilemma and that I wouldn't be able to start in two months, since my husband had just started his green card process and we didn't know how much time it would take. I flew back to Switzerland feeling hopeful but at the same time realistic. I didn't expect any job offers yet due to the situation. I felt relieved that true opportunities for a change were becoming tangible.

After a week or two had passed, to my astonishment, I received an email from the hospital where I had interviewed. They offered me the same position for July, which was seven months away! I was awestruck. For me, this was a sign of reassurance that we were moving in the right direction. The immigration process for my husband, however, would turn out not to be so easy. It seemed that we had delay after delay with our immigration paperwork. First, there was a spelling error of my name that took weeks to correct. After that, there was a problem with attributing a number for our case. Weeks turned to months, and little progress was being made. We started to doubt if this was the right thing or not. I was concerned about my job offer, since it was becoming clear that I wouldn't make it for the July start date. I emailed my HR contact at the hospital, explaining the problem. She quickly reassured me that they understood that these things could take a long time and that I would have a position as a nurse waiting for me regardless of the delay. This definitely helped reassure me. My husband was harder to convince. The significant delays were hard on him, and he doubted if we were doing the right thing. During this time, he was offered a job in Italy, working with his parents. He struggled with the dilemma that this presented.

We decided to stay put in Switzerland and to continue to see how the US immigration plan would pan out. We decided to live in the here and now and to enjoy life, even though we were going through a stressful process. Darry had recently turned thirty, and I wanted him to get what he had really wanted for years, a sports car. We purchased a twenty-year-old convertible BMW Z3 roadster. It wasn't a practical purchase, but it was definitely a fun one! We enjoyed taking that car for scenic rides in the Swiss and French Alps. We realized that life would pass us by if we constantly avoided decisions due to the "what ifs."

Finally, things were starting to move along with my husband's visa case. I had sent in all of the required documents (or so I thought), and, in my mind, I was just waiting on the visa centre to give us the green light for our visa interview date. Weeks went by. I called the centre to see what was taking so long. The woman there told me that we were missing an Italian police report and that the Swiss police report that I had sent was not the right one. I was hit once again by a disappointing blow. I felt betrayed by my own country. I couldn't understand why they made it so hard for my husband and me to make a life there together. We pressed on and obtained the missing documents, sent them to the centre, and hoped for the best. As with every step of this process, weeks went by without any news. I called the centre yet again. The woman that I talked with asked me in a condescending tone if I had two immigration cases pending. I replied, "No, just one for my husband." Again, she spoke in an even more condescending tone: "Yes, you do." I was speechless for a few seconds. What did they screw up this time? "No, there is only one case, there has only ever been one case, for my husband." "Oh, so you don't have any kids or any other family members immigrating to the US?" "No," I replied emphatically. The woman told me that she would have to send an email to a supervisor to review the problem in the system and that this would take at least a week.

A week crawled by, and, as usual, no news from the visa centre. I called again. This time, a different woman replied. She told me that my case had been sent to the supervisor for review but that it would take up to four more weeks for a reply. I couldn't take it anymore. I told the woman that there had been problem after problem with my husband's case and that it wasn't normal. I explained that I had an employer that had been waiting for me to come to the United States for over ten months. I asked if there was any way that our case could be expedited. The woman, who seemed understanding, gave me an email address I could use asking to put a rush on the case. She explained that there was no guarantee that they would accept the request. I sent an email to the address explaining our problems and asking for expedition.

This was the moment when things finally started to turn around. A few days after my email was sent, I received verification that our case was accepted for expeditious processing. We breathed some sighs of relief. After a few more days, the American Embassy in Switzerland contacted us directly and instructed us on what to do before the visa interview. We were able to collect the rest of the required documentation and notified the embassy. They scheduled my husband's visa interview immediately. This was the last thing we had to do for his immigration application.

The day of the interview came, and it went very well. My husband had everything he needed to immigrate to the United States. We were finally free from this limbo world that we lived in, where we couldn't make any definitive plans, such as starting a family or buying a house. At last we were cleared!

Do I regret the choice that I made to immigrate to Switzerland to be with my husband? The answer is no, not at all. Was it hard at times? Yes, it was very hard. But I have always believed that the hard times in life are when we grow the most. It is during these defining moments when we discover what we are made of and who we really are. It wasn't all bad, either. We were able to travel all over Switzerland and Europe, experience many different cultures and have many adventures. I was able to become pretty fluent in French, which opened a door on brand-new opportunities. I was also able to experience firsthand what immigrants go through when they abandon everything for a new life. Now that I will be moving back to my own country, I know that I will be going back changed. My views on things have evolved through my experiences as an immigrant. Things that I never thought of as being important before now have meaning. I am thankful for everything that I have done and for the people that I have met along the way. While we are not sure if we will settle in the USA indefinitely, or use it as a second residence in the future, we both agree that we will see how things go and have an open mind. I can't wait to see what the next chapter will bring.

Cheryl Lee Latter

Home Sweet Herm

I grew up in the northwest of England. My little town is right between Manchester and Liverpool, about seventeen miles away from each. Several cities and large towns are within a thirty-minute drive, but where I am from can be easily missed as you whizz down the adjacent motorway. It is the middle of everywhere and yet the middle of nowhere.

When I was a child, the next town may as well have been a million miles away. A small town makes for a very insular existence. Everyone is related, everyone knows each other's business, and most people stay there their entire lives. From an early age, all I wanted to do was get out of there. I never felt like I fit in at all.

I always dreamed of living in the country, living by the sea, somewhere with wide open spaces and no people. It made me sad to see a tree in a little square of dirt surrounded by cars and tarmac. A tree should be in a field or a wood, surrounded by other trees. I felt like those little trees, a wild thing displaced into a crowd.

My most treasured memories were rare trips to the seaside, when I would close my eyes and drink in the sound of the waves and the feel of the sand between my fingers. I was never happy in the real world, a world of exhaust and buses and grime, and would daydream about the still blue waters and soft beaches.

After I got married and had a daughter, we moved a lot. We lived in a lot of small towns and a lot of cities. It was the middle of a huge property boom, and rental houses were always getting sold out from under us. We got to the point where we were moving every six months and not even bothering to unpack.

Much as I loved England, there was nothing there for us as a young family. I went back to work when my daughter was four months old. I did the breakfast and dinner shifts in a pub, and my husband worked nights. It meant we could save money on childcare, but it also meant we never saw each other and rarely slept. Despite all our hard work, it was still difficult to keep up with bills, and some weeks I would only have £20 for a week's worth of groceries.

On winter mornings, I was up at five to wrap my daughter up in warm clothes, put her in her pram, and walk in the dark and the rain and the snow along the main road, the mile-and-a-half to work. There, I would take over from my husband for the breakfast shift and he would walk her all the way back home.

I was already familiar with Herm, having worked a couple of summer seasons there about five years earlier. The island is situated in the heart of the English Channel, ninety miles south of the UK coast and thirty miles west of France. It was, in fact, part of Normandy many centuries ago. Herm was the only place that ever truly felt like home to me. The summers were idyllic—long working hours but also fun, friends, beaches, boat trips. I loved every minute of it. On my days off, I would take long walks, drinking in the silence and the scenery, and dreading having to return to the real world.

Throughout those first difficult years of our young family, the island called out to me, and I wanted nothing more than to share it with my husband and daughter. It was a fabulous place to raise a child—no vehicles, no crime, no danger at all. The safest place in the world.

I would visit the website and read the blog every week, and every time I saw the little island children, I just knew that my daughter would fit in with them perfectly.

We were still moving a lot but desperately wanted to settle somewhere before she started school. We worked for a huge pub chain, so staff moved around a lot within the company. We generally lived in nice areas, but, as with everywhere these days, there were a lot of drugs and violent crimes, even in the good areas. There were several murders within a few years, and a young girl was killed in the woods near our house.

I still love the northwest, but I wanted to give my daughter the best start in life I possibly could, and I felt that her delicate little personality would fit somewhere with a gentler pace. Growing up in the north is hard, and we never wanted her to have to grow up fighting.

One day, when visiting the Herm website, I clicked on the recruitment section and saw that they needed a manager for the island tavern. They were looking specifically for young families to keep the school going. Without a second thought, we sent off our applications.

It seemed ironic that things happened when they did. We were finally renting a beautiful furnished house just minutes away from work, we were both nicely settled in our jobs and had great friends, we had only just found dentists and doctors we were happy with. My daughter was happy at nursery, my husband was very involved in his martial arts group, and I was able to schedule all my working hours into four long days and have three days off to write. Money was still a struggle, but we were surviving.

It felt like a big risk to maybe throw it all away.

Still, we hoped and prayed every day until we got an email stating that we were in the final two applicants for the job and they would like to fly us out for an interview. We could barely believe it. Even the worst-case scenario was that we would get a free minibreak in our favourite place, something we couldn't afford to do on our own.

Also, it didn't escape me that our interview was scheduled for October 16. It was exactly five years to the day since I had left the island after my last summer season. It seemed like it was meant to be.

To live on Herm, you have to work there. The entire island is the business, and no one is able to buy property. Approximately sixty-five people live there permanently year-round, and the island is only accessible by a twenty-minute boat journey from Guernsey. It is only a mile and a half long by half a mile wide, with one half high rocky cliff paths and the other half beautiful sandy beaches. It has one hotel, one pub, a gift shop, beach cafés, self-catering cottages and a campsite.

The island has a rich history involving monks, pirates, smugglers, Prussian royalty and Nazi invaders. It is a tiny, fascinating and utterly unique place.

It is an hour's flight from England and, on a clear day, it is possible to see right across to the coast of France, which is much closer. Herm isn't part of the UK but is part of the British Isles. It is a British Crown dependency, run by the States of Guernsey. Herm is part of the Bailiwick of Guernsey, along with the islands of Sark and Alderney. It is a place of emerald fields, sparkling blue seas and wild golden bracken.

Our interviews went well, we met lots of the island residents, and our daughter got on well with the other children. She loved the wild, wintery walks and the rock pools filled with sparkly shells and starfish. The three of us felt strongly that we could fit in and be good islanders.

On one rainy walk on the beach between interviews, I took a moment to say a little prayer to the island spirits to let us stay. I picked up a small shiny granite rock and put it in my coat pocket for luck.

Back home, we waited for a call that seemed to take forever to come, although, in reality, it was only a week.

When it finally came, it was actually bad news. The other applicants had more experience, so they had given them the job. They had all liked us and thought we would have made wonderful islanders, but that was little comfort. They promised to call if anything else came up, and I remember thinking, *I'm never going to hear from this person again.*

So, we were heartbroken, and I spent the next three days trying not to cry. I felt like that had been our only shot at moving to the place I loved so much.

Then, I had a call from my husband while I was halfway through a busy dinner shift at work. He may not have got the manager job in Herm, but he had been offered the assistant manager job, and they wanted us to move in January. I told him he'd better have said yes! And I said a silent thank you to the island spirits.

Moving day was long. We'd had a leaving party the night before, so with three hours' sleep and huge hangovers, we got the early flight from Manchester to Jersey. After waiting for several hours in Jersey, we took a tiny little Trislander plane to Guernsey. The weather was awful, so it was a very bumpy and rickety ride over the little islands, but it was fun to watch the tiny boats beneath us, leaving their little trails of foam behind them.

I was very proud of my daughter. She had only just turned four, but she didn't complain one bit, even though she understood we were leaving everything behind for good. I had promised her that her cuddly toys were on their way to the new house, and that was good enough for her.

It was growing dark by the time we got on the last Herm boat of the day. It felt like every island resident was on that boat, all talking and smiling and asking questions. I felt exhausted and terrified, and I just painted a big smile on my face and tried not to yawn.

We had been given a self-catering place right next to our new house to stay in for a few days while we got organized, and they had put milk, bread, coffee, etc. in the kitchen for us. There was even a huge potted plant on the doorstep as a welcome gift.

We were so excited to look at our new place that we ditched our bags and went straight round there. Our furniture was scheduled to come on a cargo boat a few days later, so our little flat was empty. It was much smaller than the home we'd left, just a square cut into living room/kitchen, two bedrooms and a bathroom. We were just happy to see a bathtub and a little wooden patio. It was all we needed.

I won't deny that the first few months were hard, despite living in paradise. It was winter, and in my memory, it rained constantly those first few months. My husband was at work every day, and without work and nursery to structure us, my daughter and I hung around the house a lot. You can only go out for walks in the rain and wind so many times a day. Most of the other children were of school age, so there was no nursery or day care.

The island generates all its own power, so in those early days we weren't even allowed electric kettles. Tumble dryers are still not allowed, and you have to live here for seven years before you can have a dishwasher. I felt like a pioneer woman boiling water in a pan on the gas hob to make a cup a tea. It was all part of the fun, though.

We didn't have satellite or cable TV, or a phone, or even any money to begin with. The company had fronted us the money for flights and removals, and we were paying them back. Twice a week, there was an extra lunchtime boat, so we would go to the library in Guernsey just for a change of scenery that didn't cost anything. I tried hard to structure our days and be creative, but I found it hard not to work.

Even now, I haven't forgotten those first few months. I always have empathy for new mothers who move here and do my best to help them to settle in. And we are still always loyal to that library that gave us a cosy place to go, out of the wind and rain. In fact, my daughter, who is now fourteen, volunteers there every Saturday.

We did all we could to be good islanders. Those first few years, we went to everything. Every week there was a Friday Club at the pub, where all the residents got together for dinner. My husband was always working, and my daughter would go off and play with the other children. I inevitably would end up sitting alone. I went anyway. I wanted to do all I could to fit in.

By spring, things got easier. The businesses were opening up, so I picked up work wherever I could, even though I had to take my daughter with me. By July, I had three cleaning jobs and was writing a weekly column for the local paper. I had even started to plan out a book about the island. Now that I was out and about more, friendships began to grow and get stronger, and our days had a good routine.

We have several beautiful beaches just minutes away from our house, and we always felt so lucky to be able to go there after work and school every day. There are also gorgeous walks along the cliff paths, lots of places of historical interest, and a vast grassy common filled with dolmens and wild rabbits. People always wonder what there is to do on such a tiny island, but the ever-changing nature around us never gets dull.

Once school started that September, time began to fly by. We all began to find our niche. In a community this small, you really do get out what you put in. Being able to be at the school gate every day and volunteer to help out with fetes and visits, whilst also working, was a privilege I wouldn't necessarily have had in the UK. The school was in the same little courtyard as the cottages I was cleaning, so I was only ever minutes away and could hear my daughter in the playground. We went home for lunch together every day, or she came to the cottage if I was busy.

Most years, there are around seven children in the little school, from ages four to eleven. They are all taught in one room, with one teacher, and they go to a bigger school in Guernsey one day a week to get used to being around other children.

The children have amazing opportunities in their unique school environment. They are on the radio and local TV a lot, and they were in the National Union of Teachers magazine and on the cover of *Drama* magazine. My daughter has met Prince Charles and Camilla once and Prince Edward and Sophie twice. They have had trips on Sunseeker yachts and a whole-school trip to London, where they got to do a workshop at the Globe Theatre. They learn Shakespeare from age four and often go out into the woods to draw bluebells or pick blackberries.

Plus, they get to see their parents throughout the day, or at least see them working through the school window, which not a lot of children are lucky enough to do.

It is an idyllic, perfect seaside childhood where they are safe from the dangers of the outside world.

By the end of our third year, I was running the self-catering cottages, and by our fourth year, my husband had moved on to the outdoor team. For the first time in our family life, our daughter had both parents home every evening.

Although part of our job is to make things seem effortless, we do work very hard and are always on duty. It is a regular thing to get stopped and quizzed by strangers on the history and day-to-day running of the island, and I've lost count of the times that someone has randomly wandered into my office, or even my house, looking for somewhere else. Our business depends on guests and day-trippers, and from March to December there can be hundreds on the island at any given time. The off season technically runs from October to

March, but January and February are our quietest months, where we get to slow down a bit and have our own holidays.

Very often, residents only stay for five years or so, so things are constantly changing around us, with new people coming and going all the time. Things never get stagnant or boring because the community is always changing.

In nine days' time, it will be ten years since we moved to our paradise isle. I still run the cottages and work as a journalist and local author. My husband works outdoors and is a special constable and first aider. Our daughter is now at high school and boards in Guernsey through the week, coming home for weekends and holidays.

There are downsides, of course. The winters can be hard, especially if boats are cancelled with bad weather. We can literally run out of food, and your friends and neighbours become very important if you need to borrow milk or bread for a couple of days. Everyone is very good at sharing and bartering, and we don't let anyone go without. And it is very important to be flexible with appointments and holidays because sometimes you just might not make it off the island at all.

Being separated from our daughter through the week was very hard at first, as she was only nine when she first went. It has got easier as she has got older, but I do envy the other mums in Guernsey being able to do the school run every day. She lives with an amazing host family, though, and is able to go to an excellent school. I am able to give her all the opportunities I didn't have. We appreciate our weekends together more, as well, and see few teenage tantrums because of it.

In one way, I feel like we have crammed so much into our ten years here, never complacent, always grateful for the opportunities we have been given and the wonderful environment we have raised our child in. The island has taken us in and given us a wonderful home and many fabulous memories.

On the other hand, it only seems like five minutes since we got off that boat, tired, bedraggled and terrified that we may have made a huge mistake and thrown away a good life in England.

Living here isn't forever. Your life here lasts only as long as the job. No one can retire here. We have no future plans, no money, nowhere else we want to be. Everything we own is within these square little walls on a little patch of granite in the middle of the channel.

One day, we will have no choice but to pack up again and head off into the sunset, but where that will take us only time will tell.

Agnese Accapezzato

Where is Home for You?

At the airport, my flight is delayed, and I wander around the numerous restaurants and souvenir shops. I decide to buy some chocolate candies, and after assisting me, a kind cashier asks, "Are you flying home?"

For a moment, I stare at him, trying to figure out where I'm actually going. At first, I think that maybe my flight has been cancelled or redirected and that is why I can't seem to find the answer. Then, I realize this has nothing to do with my flight. I know exactly where the airplane will take me; I just don't know whether I should call that place home.

A few months ago, I moved to Brussels, in Belgium, and that is where I am supposed to fly back to. It's not that I don't like Brussels or that I don't feel at home in this city yet; I hesitate because when the cashier hits me with that question, I suddenly realize I have been migrating from one place I used to call home to another and I still haven't figured out where I want to settle down and have a place I can call home for the rest of my life.

In the last four years, I have lived in six different countries and at least seven apartments with eight roommates; I have travelled many places and met people from all over the world.

I was born in Italy, in a small town where I never felt comfortable living. I always felt like I didn't belong there and that there was so much more outside, waiting for me to discover it. I still remember the first English class at primary school: I was so fascinated by the fact that we could communicate the same things in a different language, and for my birthday that year, I asked my mum to take me to London. She was afraid of flying, so I never went there till I was thirteen and I started to go to colleges in the UK for a few weeks every summer to take English courses. That was definitely the time of year I looked forward to the most, far away from the artichoke plantations of my land. Growing up in a small town means that you get to know everybody and people get to judge you on what they think they know about you. I was tired of always seeing the same people and the same places, and I wanted to explore new, exciting horizons. After graduating from high school, I left my hometown to go to university in Rome, where I spent incredible years, but I still had the desire to move somewhere outside my country.

In 2013, I applied for a scholarship which led me to the University of Washington in Seattle for an exchange program, and I finally achieved my dream. After that experience as an international student, everything changed. I realized I could only be completely myself when I was living abroad, speaking a language different from my mother tongue with people who were not from my country and only judged me for who I really was: an independent woman. I felt free, respected and appreciated. I also figured out that after graduation from university, I should look for a job in an international environment where I could meet people who shared my same ideas and aspirations.

The summer before my graduation ceremony, I moved to Lyon in France in order to learn another language to increase my chances of getting a job with an international organization. Once again, I fell in love with the city and its people. During the first two weeks, I couldn't speak a single word of French, and almost nobody around me could speak English. That forced me to practice and allowed me to learn the language even faster. Eventually, this short-lived experience left me with the immeasurable gift of being able to speak a new language.

After that, I moved back to Rome to complete a second master's degree before eventually migrating again, this time to Switzerland. I got an internship in Geneva, and I initially thought I would only stay there for six months. When I first arrived there, I didn't really like the city. I thought it was too expensive and too boring, but after only three months, my idea completely changed. I discovered a beautifully diverse city, I met amazing friends, and I realized there were many opportunities to pursue an international career. I worked hard and eventually got selected by the International Organization for Migration (IOM) for an internship with the International Migration Law Unit, whose key objective is to encourage dissemination and understanding of the international legal standards that govern migration and provide protection of the rights of migrants. I stayed in Geneva for six more months, and I started to feel like I had finally found a place I could call home, with people I could consider my second family. But then everything changed, quite unexpectedly.

I was offered a contract with IOM in Djibouti, in Africa, and I decided to move there because I thought it was the right time in my life to have this kind of field experience, on both a professional and a personal level. I was very sad to leave Geneva, but at the same time I was excited to embark on this new adventure. Moving to this tiny country in the Horn of Africa, about which I had so little information, gave me a mixed feeling of excitement and fear. The first days were really tough; I struggled so much to find housing, and I moved from one hotel to another before I eventually managed to find an apartment. My new home was very conveniently located near my office. My street, like every other street in Djibouti except for the main one, was just a dirt road. On the left, there was a fruit stand and a small bakery, where I used to buy a typical bread with raisins and honey. On the other side, a drug store and a few other shops. The chaotic city centre, with its colourful buildings, crowded market and baby goats at every corner, was just a short drive away. All around, there was white sand and the crystal-clear sea of the Gulf of Aden. From day one, I integrated very well with local colleagues and had a great professional experience. Being a woman alone in Djibouti was not always easy, and I could read concern in other expats' eyes each time I told them I was living and going around all by myself. But it was surely a life-changing and rewarding experience. For the first time in my life, I felt alone and far away from all my loved ones, but at the same time I was thankful for the opportunity I had been given because it allowed me to focus more deeply on my long-term goals and objectives. I had found a little group of friends, I enjoyed the sun shining every day, and I would have stayed there for a longer period but my contract expired and my new job brought me back to Europe, where I'm currently living.

I'm based in Brussels, but I get to travel for work very often, especially to Tallinn, the capital of Estonia, which I had never been to before. I spent several days there recently, and, thanks to my colleagues, I also got to discover the culture, the food and the lifestyle of that new place in my personal world map. Brussels is a vibrant and international city where I feel comfortable, but I don't know how long I will stay here, and I don't even know how long I would like to stay, if I had the chance to decide right now.

The only thing I know for sure is that Italy is my unique homeland. Italy means family; Italy is everything I ever loved or hated. It now represents the place I go to if I want to be on vacation or see my family. Italy is the blood I have running through my veins that keeps me going and reminds me why I act in a certain way or why I use gestures when I speak, or why I will always need to look for some type of ingredients at the grocery store. Italy is a country that I love even more and feel more proud of when I'm not there but that I still don't want to live in.

I would say I am a migrant worker because I chose to be one. I always dreamed of having a job that would allow me to travel and discover different cultures. At this point in my life, I feel very grateful for the experiences I have. Getting to know people and places all over the world has enriched me in a way that is difficult to explain. The love and happiness, the struggle and loneliness, have made me the person I am today: a citizen of the world. I feel at home everywhere I go, but at the same time I feel like I will never be completely at home again because there is always someone or somewhere that will be missed in my heart.

Lorna Jane Harvey

Wine, Tractors and Foreigners

Saturday morning, we sat on a café's terrace and drank strong coffee and ate warm croissants au chocolat. The château d'Yverdon, a thirteenth-century castle, loomed over us and the cobblestone square. Arms filled with fresh produce, locals stopped at the bustling cafés that had spread their tables, chairs and parasols in the ancient square. The market ambled away from the square down a long, cobbled street. Rough hands worked quickly and efficiently, weighing an array of orange, purple, red, yellow, white and brown root vegetables. Salads, cabbages and chards crowded shiny tomatoes and peppers. Berries and plums filled dainty baskets in front of the coarse vegetables. Fresh scents of grandmothers' kitchens and sweet black earth overwhelmed the senses. A mushroom verifier stood in front of the mushroom stall. Amateur mushroom-hunters brought small baskets of mushrooms they'd picked and asked for the expert's approval before they dared eat them. Curry prickled my nostrils as I passed the Eastern stall, with its matching Eastern salesman, who shouted the names of his spices in Arabic. Glistening olives and kumquats, dried figs and apricots tempted us. I bought a bag of apples from a ruddy-faced elderly man, and we headed home for a lunch of strong Gruyère cheese with warm bread.

The afternoon slipped by lazily as we sipped crisp white Fendant wine on the terrace. Three green and yellow fields away, there was the village of Subsilva, to which we belonged. I could make out large farmhouses and the sharp belltower that emerged out of the mangle of tiled roofs. We tried to cool off as the day grew hotter. We ate ice cream and slept off the heat behind closed shutters, but woke even hotter and draped cold wet towels around our necks and lay lethargically on the deck. Except for the cicadas buzzing in the vines, the insects and birds had disappeared quietly in the heat.

Distant bells struck five o'clock, and somewhere beyond, sheep rang the small bells around their necks, giving the countryside a constant soft ringing sound. It was the soothing sound of green pastures and cheese. Behind me, the vines shimmered in the breeze. Above them was a stone that marked the limit of Subsilva and the village of Champvent, where I grew up. Twelve airplanes silently drew white lines in the sky. A few parachuters dropped to the ground; one screamed in delight.

As the day ended, a nightingale sang delicately from the forest. The farmers harvested many of their fields, and the grapes waited to be picked. I felt as if I were on a castle's terrace, because of the commanding, sweeping view of the valley and far-off villages. Like a fire in the distance, a full orange moon rose over the mountain. The air cooled as evening finally came. The scents of my childhood wafted around. Scents of turned earth, hay, apples, foxes and dry leaves. I was happy to be here. It made a certain kind of sense.

Two months before, we had become migrants when we moved from Vancouver Island in Canada to Switzerland. We came to Switzerland for our children to learn French, for a new experience for my husband, and because I still missed my childhood home, even though I had left Switzerland eighteen years earlier.

We landed in Geneva with a tingling sense of newness. Our daughter, Elise, began to cry. She'd been homeless for a few weeks as we travelled east, far too long for a little six-year-old, and this, this horrid place, was the final blow. She wanted to go home. Except that she had no home, and that made her cry even harder. Elise was a forward, dynamic and witty child with a big smile and a mop of tangled blonde hair. Her world crumbled when we told her of our decision to move, and her tantrums were frequent—she hated the idea of Switzerland and the French language. Her eight-year-old brother, Philippe, was less outspoken but mostly just observed silently as his world crumbled and reshaped.

We hobbled into the underground parking lot and found our rental car. After a forty-five-minute drive under an undistinguishable sky, the hard-edged city had disappeared and we left the highway to drive over hilly country roads surrounded by angular yellow and green fields, occasionally separated by small, dark forests. In the distance, a thin strip of blue sky highlighted the Alps' white tips. Clusters of stone houses with red tiled roofs grew out of the fields, like porcini mushrooms in a meadow.

We arrived at our new home. Well, at the place we'd rented. One of the farmhands pointed to a big blue tractor caked in mud. Out hopped a young man with a smiling round face, matching body and dark brown hair, who introduced himself as Pierre. He led us to a pink villa next to the farm. Lizards scurried across the walkway, which was strewn with yellow grass clippings. Flower blossoms peered through weeds in the garden beds on the edge of the path. Pained moaning came from a nearby barn.

"What's that noise?" I asked.

John answered, through his thick Vaudois accent, "That is a cat in heat." We followed him wordlessly with only the sound of our footsteps to mask the cat's moaning.

A childhood friend from the next village had found the place for us to rent, but we only had vague details about it. We just knew it was temporary and inexpensive.

Pierre opened the front door, and the smell of decaying furniture, stale food and old habits poured out of the house. The entrance was tiled with brown lozenges, as was the long living room. The orange wooden furniture was oversized and oppressive. An elaborately spider-webbed oak buffet frowned over a dark elongated table. A side buffet rested against a wall like a forlorn coffin. Dusty and stained, stacked floral couches balanced at odd angles. Peeling wallpaper showed marks of where a dozen frames used to hang. The kitchen was brown, as was every other room in the house, except for the master bedroom, which was carefully decorated with flowery blue wallpaper and had a powder-blue silk-and-tassel lampshade.

"It's nice," my husband said with such a strong Quebec accent that the young farmer had to stop and think about what Jacques had just said.

"Ah. You should have seen it two days ago. It wasn't like this! We've cleaned it up!" he exclaimed proudly, and then added, "But there's no hot water. Not yet, anyway. We're waiting for the oil to be delivered."

Philippe and Elise, bleary-eyed, followed silently. Once Pierre finished showing us through the brown mansion, he left and we looked outside. The yard was huge, and we had a fantastic view over fields and hills and distant mountains. We dropped our suitcases on the living room floor and pulled out our blow-up mattresses. The kids ran around the house as thin spiders scattered out of the way.

The children, utterly spent, soon dropped to sleep. We put them to bed in a room with two single bed frames. They seemed happy to not be alone, even though the place had enough bedrooms that we could have separated them. I walked around our villa, exhausted but so happy to be there.

Geographically, Switzerland could fit 240 times into Canada. It's a country that can easily be driven across in a day. Since there are nearly eight million inhabitants, population is fairly dense. With a few exceptions, most of the communities or villages are within commuting range to a city. The biggest difference between the two countries is proximity. In Canada, I found that living in a small town meant being physically removed from a city by hundreds of kilometres. Here, I lived in the country yet conveniently less than half an hour from a major city.

A week after we arrived, school started. I wrote Philippe and Elise a note that said their names, birth dates, address and phone number, and that they spoke English and no French. In the early morning, Elise and I trembled together at the bus stop across the road from our house.

"I don't like this, Mummy. I don't feel right anymore. If they make fun of me, I'll just walk out."

"No, you won't. You won't know how to find your way home. Elise, please, just go for the morning. We'll talk about it at lunchtime. It'll be okay."

Elise frowned, glared at me—the cause of all her problems.

"I don't like your country," she said as the mini school bus finally pulled up. The same driver who, twenty-five years before, used to take me to school was behind the wheel. Philippe caught the same bus thirty minutes later, now on the older kids' round.

"I'll be fine. You don't need to worry, Mummy. Just tell me how to say, 'I don't understand,' in French again?" He gave me a rough hug, then distanced himself when he saw the bus. He looked at the bus, looked back at me blankly, then climbed on. A busload of quiet children stared. The door slid shut and the bus pulled away.

My husband went to work with the car. Home alone with no phone, internet or car, I contemplated my dirty, spidery house. The hill behind our house loomed as childhood memories rushed back to me.

"I chose to be here. I wanted this," I heard my frightened whisper say as a chill ran through my body.

People have always moved around the world and left their imprints beyond their own lifetimes. These migration imprints form our history, a history that is rich with tradition, architecture, food and languages. But not all migrants make strong imprints in their new land. Some quickly assimilate to their new surroundings and blend. I'd like to think I'm that kind of migrant.

I suppose my early childhood was like many, or at least like many would like. I lived with my parents and my sister in a four-hundred-year-old renovated house. We had two cats and a dog. We lived next door to my grandparents in a small Swiss village where everyone seemed to be friendly. We travelled to England once or twice a year to visit my other grandparents, and the family dynamics appeared to be healthy, happy and conflict-free.

When I was in elementary school, my Swiss grandmother died of cancer. An inheritance war ensued, as my grandparents' farm was in my grandmother's name only. It ended with my uncle winning all the inheritance in court. Fairly soon afterwards, my grandfather committed suicide. I heard the gunshot.

Within a couple of years, we immigrated to Canada.

When I moved from Switzerland to Canada in 1990, I was nearly thirteen years old. I wasn't given much of a choice, but my father sold the idea as a fantastic adventure to my sister and me. My parents, my sister, my dog and I flew to Montreal. We bought a Jeep and drove over four thousand kilometres across Canada. We settled in a small rural town in British Columbia. The children in my high school, at first curious to hear my French and British accent, soon mocked me, and I blended in as fast as possible. Within two years, I sounded as Canadian as anyone else in my class. I hated that my parents packed strange lunches for me because it showed everyone that I was a foreigner. When I opened my lunch bag and saw a slice of bread and a cold sausage, I closed it quietly and said I wasn't hungry.

I was a foreigner in Canada for five years, until I moved to Vancouver Island for university. There, people assumed I was Canadian, and I didn't volunteer that I wasn't. I even officially became a Canadian citizen then.

Countries such as Canada are referred to as cultural mosaics, where a blend of languages, ethnic groups and cultures live alongside each other fairly successfully within a society. Immigration has shaped Canada. This ideal of multiculturalism is usually contrasted with assimilation or social integration or "melting pots'" (as in the United States of America). Switzerland's approach seems to be more one of assimilation, where the population is expected to base their values on the Constitution, tolerance and respect.

In Switzerland, it shocked me when people said, "I love your accent! A bit of Québécois . . . with English lilts. So sweet!"

I shook my head and glared. I refused to admit that I had an accent. I came from here. I learned French here. Everywhere I'd spoken in French outside of Switzerland, people said I had an accent. A Swiss accent. So to be told that I had an accent here was an insult. If I had an accent in Switzerland, it meant that I was a foreigner. I never expected to be an "other" here. I thought I was one of them.

Switzerland is a country where a quarter of the residents are foreign. A country that has prided itself on its neutrality and its refugee acceptance program. The culture, which has historically encompassed foreigners, is constantly modified by global changes, modernization and, of course, by foreigner input.

Some question at what point a culture can no longer sustain itself because the outside influences have grown overpowering, a sort of distortion or denaturing of national identity. There has been a recent wave of political discourse around "protecting the Swiss culture" that has been deemed by many as racist. Culture as we know it is not permanent. It is and always has been, similarly to language, in a constant state of change. This often adds richness to its nature. Culture is valuable because it has and will always change. When it stops changing, it becomes stagnant, obsolete, uninteresting. But it is difficult to accept the change as it happens.

At the village supper for new inhabitants, Subsilva welcomed three newcomers that year: a third cousin's wife, my husband and me (strangely, children didn't count). The mayor and a handful of men and women who served on the village council greeted us vigorous-ly, some with strong handshakes and others with three kisses. Rosé wine from the vines behind our house, served with fluted crackers, softened the more rigid municipal members. Two eighteen-year-olds had also been invited to be welcomed as adults into the village. One of the municipal councillors asked us if we planned to stay.

"Oui, pour le moment," I answered. Yes, for the time being. That was the noncommittal local answer to any uncomfortable question —an expression that frustrated me daily. Is the furnace fixed? Oui, pour le moment. The pipe is still leaking. Are we just going to leave it like that? Oui, pour le moment . . .

We newcomers made an important numerical addition to a sleepy village of 187 people. Related to nearly a quarter of the people in the village, we couldn't be considered as complete strangers. But we had extra appeal since we'd just arrived from another country. Some even thought us a little exotic. Certainly mysterious. Somehow, we'd ended up living in the abandoned house on the edge of the village, the house that no one else had been allowed to rent until we came along. We became an unsolvable puzzle to the villagers.

At the newcomers' supper, we moved on to white wine and huge quantities of cheese fondue. The mayor made a welcome speech into which she wove the importance of formalities, especially with regard to *tu* and *vous*. These new adults would be called *vous* from now on, as they had reached the legal voting age, and although it might be difficult, it was important that everyone abide by the traditions.

I slipped away early to let the babysitter go home, but my husband stayed on happily. He was oblivious to the subtleties of formality and so happily said *tu* to most people—but he did it with such sincerity that no one seemed to be offended, and Jacques soon felt at home and content in Switzerland.

When I arrived home, it was midnight. The kids slept peacefully, and the babysitter rushed to get her shoes and jacket when she saw me.

"I'll walk you home," I offered. She smiled, glad not to walk home alone. We walked up the dark path towards her house under a clear but moonless night. Vibrant stars shimmered in the sky. We chit-chatted amiably all the way to her house, and then I walked home alone. I listened to the nearby forest. I knew this forest well. As a child, it was my playground. I kissed my kindergarten sweetheart under these trees. I hid behind the tall trees and cried when I had to leave for Canada. I could almost run with my eyes closed up the paths that all led to each other. It was a maze full of treasures and sweetness in the day, but an unfriendly veil settled over the wood at night. Sounds were distorted, branches cracked and footsteps padded across the dry leaves; it felt as though eyes watched from the shadows.

I suddenly became aware that I was vulnerable all alone in the dark, shadowless night. Boars roamed the forest, although I'd never actually seen any, and strange people sometimes lurked—them I had seen. I stomped like a man to appear stronger, less vulnerable. I looked around and thought I saw something move on the edge of the black forest. I shuddered, started to jog, ran all the way home to safety.

Months passed, and we adapted to the routine of family life. We returned to Canada for Christmas. We skated on shallow frozen ponds, built an igloo, skied, ate and drank too much and generally had a merry time. Once we were back in Switzerland, the gentle pace of Canada soon vanished. A few hours after we arrived, the children went to school and I groggily made my way to the grocery store. Slowly, I walked down aisles of turnips, cabbages and potatoes. Women pushed me, shoved their carts into mine, generally crowded me. I treasure my personal space, and as uptight women pushed into it, I clenched my jaw and widened my shoulders. Oblivious, they only pushed more.

The pace is always quicker in Switzerland; people walk faster and shop faster. After being away from it, I thought it seemed worse. I refused to make eye contact with my aggressors but instead let my cart get bullied. I felt on the verge of tears by the time I arrived at the check-out counter, but I told myself it was jetlag. Unlike in Canada, I had to pack my own groceries. The cashier made me understand I had to rush to get out of the way as the next person's groceries started to pile up behind mine. After I paid, I hurried to the end of the counter and frantically packed my groceries. I set one of my full bags on the edge of the counter, and the next woman in line pushed past me and knocked the bag to the ground. Enough! I'd gone from near tears to anger. I wanted to shout at the stupid woman, but instead I just stared at her, and she laughed. I came very near to slapping her, but I just bent down and picked up my scattered groceries.

Time has a funny way of adjusting our perceptions. Within a few weeks, the rushed attitude of the Swiss seemed normal to us again, and we went back to being content with their ways.

The north of England, only a long day's journey from Switzerland, was strewn with the other half of my extended family. After living in Western Canada for nearly two decades with no family beyond my sister and my parents, Europe felt almost crowded with relations. We drove and sailed to meet them.

I had fond childhood memories of the drive from two decades earlier, when we'd visit my grandparents in the north of England. Now, our white Renault Laguna wound over the small roads between

Switzerland and France and soon we cruised over the freeways, well on our way to England. In France, we stopped for breakfast in a charming stone village, where the pace was refreshingly slow after the fast roads. We found a bakery tucked away on a side street. Even though we'd only been driving a couple of hours, I was acutely aware of my Swiss French accent. The lady behind the counter pretended not to understand me, and so I repeated myself. The people who had come in behind me already formed a queue, and I could hear them chuckle. But the croissants tasted delicious, far better than the best croissants in Switzerland.

We drove most of the day and then reached Calais and drove on to the ferry. After a meal of greasy fish and chips with mushy peas, we watched the White Cliffs of Dover appear through the mist. On the outer deck, I leaned on the ship's white and brown rails, rusty from years of stormy waves washing over them. Life rafts creaked as they swung gently in the slight wind. A fair-haired family dressed in matching yellow rain gear pointed excitedly at the fast-approaching island. Tears fell down the woman's pale face. I imagined they were migrants going to a promised land, or perhaps returning home after many years away. They were, it seemed, on an emotional journey that would change their lives forever.

We arrived at my aunt's house at one o'clock in the morning after a horrendous day driving through rain and getting lost on small backroads.

The following morning, we drove further north, along a wild stretch of coast where the sea beats into the cliffs incessantly and shapes the vegetation and even the people. The car's engine complained, shook, groaned, threatened to die. On the outskirts of Scarborough, in the small town of Seamer, the car limped into the Renault garage.

"You're tourists?" the mechanic asked as he stared at our car's Swiss licence plates. The question seemed so ridiculous that I truthfully answered, with a Canadian accent, 'No, I'm British,' to which he burst out laughing.

Behind the garage, in the fields, an old ruin watched us patiently. Only the stone archway remained. A few sheep kept the grass trimmed around the base of the thousand-year-old remnants. Nearby, a moss-covered Anglican church was framed by a wild-looking cemetery. At first glance, they were much the same as many other Anglican church grounds in Yorkshire, but the graveyard's perimeter was lined with ancient tombstones. They leaned against each other like books on a library shelf. Ivy crowded around them. We made a game of trying to find the oldest one and glimpsed messages of love and sorrow that dated four and five hundred years. I searched the headstones for my ancestors' names, men and women who roamed this land hundreds of years before, but I found no Robsons among them.

My ancestors, the Robsons, arrived as Norse Vikings nearly a millennium ago. The Robsons are part of the Gunn clan, whose territory straddled England and Scotland. Their motto was Aut pax aut bellum (either peace or war). Stranded in my maternal homeland, I felt like this was a good place to be; it was almost as if the land knew me. Maybe I was, I realized, an eternal migrant whose broad roots could never let me feel fully at home anywhere.

The car was repaired by early afternoon. We enjoyed seeing my cousins. Their ways, so different from ours, seemed enticing. Their food, their speech, their manners, even their appearance was so completely different from ours. The television permeated most of the English homes we visited. We usually ate meals with our English relatives on our laps, rather than at tables.

"They sound like people in the movies, Mummy," Elise whispered.

"Your English family, they're pretty nice," my husband said as we started the long drive home. "They seem settled—happy."

Home after a long drive through snow and countless tolls, I felt more Swiss than ever before. Several times during the holiday in England, we had been made to understand that in Britain, we were foreigners, and that my British passport meant little to them if I spoke with a North American accent. It seems so trivial that pronunciation of the same words can make humanity accept or refuse others, allow them in or push them away as "others."

Nevertheless, I was home in Switzerland after a holiday, and that meant piles of laundry. The house was a mess. I worried someone might come by for a visit and see my shortcomings as a homemaker. Except that I didn't really care to be that kind of homemaker. I made a home, but I had work to do, kids to care for, a life to live. The dust and scattered toys would come back again and again. As long as my home was clean, welcoming, and filled with love and joy, that was enough for me. If there was a pile of clean laundry on the couch waiting to be folded and a dusty shelf or two, I didn't really care. Or I shouldn't have cared, but I was always aware of how meticulous and critical many of the Swiss women could be. And when I write "women," I'm not being sexist. I didn't know many Swiss men in the villages nearby who did these tasks. Single men usually got their mothers to do the dirty work. The women appeared to be responsible for keeping the homes and gardens clean and tidy and productive, and provisioned with groceries and ironed clothes. At all times, their homes appeared impeccable. Swiss women's obsession with *propre en ordre* (clean and tidy) baffles me. This is particularly the case with my parents' generation, the fifty-plus-year-olds, where even underwear is ironed. When I tell them I purposely buy clothes that don't need ironing, they look disappointed and sometimes offer to do my ironing for me.

"Well, surely your husband needs his work shirts ironed," they invariably add.

"He irons his own shirts. I have other things to do. We both work, we look after our own clothes."

A look of shock, then disdain, settles on their faces, and I'm labelled as unfit. They display their lives, it seems, in homes that could pose for domesticity advertisements. Dirt and messes never stain their thresholds. It makes me laugh, mostly, but there's a little nagging feeling that perhaps I'm incompetent.

Gardening is frequently regarded as an extension of the inside of the home. In a good Swiss garden, the lawn is cut weekly, but never on Sundays or at lunchtime, since that is against the rules. Our acre-sized lawn intimidated us when we first arrived at the house. My husband cut a couple of strips of grass on either side of the driveway. The rest, we thought, could look like a hay field for all we cared.

Soon, a few women in the village told me about ticks.

"The ticks in this valley are *mauvais* (bad). The ticks give illnesses. The ticks are in long grass. You should cut your grass."

Or, sometimes, more directly: "The old people who lived in your house before they went into a home, well, they kept that place looking perfect. They'd be so upset to see it now."

Even people in the next village made a few comments. I finally decided to cut the lawn myself. The mower chugged through thick grass. I could feel the eyes of the neighbour and his employees on me as the engine slowed on the longest grass. They disapproved. I refused to look up. I was going to get through it.

A friend from the village came round for a drink and looked thoughtfully outside.

"You've hayed, I see," he said, smiling.

I didn't answer and pretended I hadn't heard. There was an awkward silence, so I said, "It's a lot of lawn to cut . . ."

"There are some who take good care of their garden and there are some who don't take quite such good care of their garden," he said sternly.

Next to the house, there was a pile of branches as big as a car. As we cleaned up our garden, we piled the branches by the side of the orchard. As it became larger, I began to ask Jacques what to do with it.

"Ask Pierre to take it away . . ." he answered vaguely.

One morning, fog coated the land. I took fire-starter gel and a lighter to the pile of branches. I wasn't sure if I was allowed to make an open fire, but since the ground was damp and the fog hid any smoke, I lit the pile. The fire grew quickly, and clouds oozed from it. The fog lifted all of a sudden, revealing blue sky, sunshine and thick, billowing smoke. The fire began to lick the long grass in the orchard. I hit the flames with a shovel, spread out the branches and drenched the fire. The pile of branches hadn't shrunk much.

Not only was I deficient in housekeeping, but it seemed I wouldn't be deemed a competent gardener, either. The villagers probably wished to tell me, "Go home, you Canadian brute!"

Before we arrived in Switzerland, Philippe and Elise spoke only a handful of French words. They now had a solid base of French, but they still struggled with new words and complicated instructions. As their first Swiss school year came to an end, the teachers meticulously organized field trips, sports days and many other special events. Philippe's grade-three teacher decided that she would not write down the instructions for sports day; instead, she was counting on her students to take responsibility and remember. Philippe came home and said, "There's a thing tomorrow. I have to take the bus in the village early."

"What time?"

"A bit earlier than school usually starts. I shouldn't take my school bus to school, but I have to walk to the village and catch the big bus from there. But before I leave, you have to call a phone number. One-eight-zero-zero or nine-six-zero-zero or one-nine-zero-zero, I think. Someone will tell you if the thing is on. If it doesn't rain. If it's on, you have to pack a picnic for me, and I won't come home at lunch. We'll go straight to our singing practice in Yverdon. If it's not on, we go to school in the morning and come home for lunch but have to go back to school early to catch a bus for song practice. Oh yeah, we're in a concert with an orchestra next week. And I have to bring a bathing suit. I think. But the teacher said yes and then no and then yes. And a towel. Just in case."

"Just in case what?"

"I don't know," he answered, and his face melted. He ran to his room and cried.

I phoned the teacher to get the story straight. The next day, Philippe was told off because he asked his mummy to figure it out for him. He had to understand all by himself now.

Many immigrant children held the label of disfavoured students —meaning that their parents did not speak French (or German or Italian or Romansch, depending on the official language of the area of Switzerland in which they lived). Special classes received these immigrants and asylum-seekers, separating them from "the others" and making it difficult to integrate at first. Since my children were "favoured" enough to have parents who spoke French, they attended a regular class but, unfortunately, with teachers who had little or no training to deal with foreign-language students.

When I sat in the same classroom two decades before, my teacher received a Portuguese immigrant student by calling him a donkey (which implies a stupid person in French). Fortunately, even after the teacher drew a donkey on the blackboard to illustrate the newcomer's idiocy, it seemed a donkey had no ill association in Portugal, and the boy was spared the humiliation.

When Elise returned from school, Philippe sat on his bed, sadly lacking motivation to play.

"What's wrong, Philippe?" his sister asked.

"Nothing. I hate school. I hate my teacher. And I hate French," he replied angrily.

"I have an idea!" Elise said brightly, and the two set to making a little cork boat in Philippe's room.

Once it was finished, Elise asked, "Can we launch it?"

We walked down the fields to the Mujon, a tiny canal, and launched the ship with much ceremony. As I turned away, I overheard Elise say, "Maybe it'll make it to the ocean. Maybe even to Vancouver Island, and then our friends in Canada will find it."

It hurt to hear because they still missed their friends in Canada. I smiled and nodded. They were happy, convinced the little boat would act as a sort of messenger across rivers and oceans, and that seemed to be enough to get through a few more days of living in Switzerland.

Nearly two years passed after we arrived in Switzerland. In the forest behind our house, I sat on a log next to my bike while Elise and Philippe took little jumps over stumps they'd arranged as an obstacle course. Hundreds of birds sang loudly from the trees. A swallow landed by my side, then took fright when she realized I wasn't a tree. Tender green shoots lightened the tips of the tree branches. Vague sounds of a haying tractor drifted from a distant field. I smelled a fox but couldn't see him.

Shooting started on the nearby range. No matter how hard I tried to ignore it, it had shattered my peace. We biked away, down the hill and out of the forest.

The château de Champvent stood patiently on the edge of the hill, with wisps of fog clinging to its four towers. The uninhabited castle looked like it belonged in a fairy tale. It was said to be a rich widow's holiday home, but its shutters remained shut for all but three weeks a year.

We biked down to our village's playground and swung long enough to become dizzy. The children laughed.

"I like this place," Elise confided.

The scent of rapeseed flowers permeated the air. The fields around us shimmered with brilliant yellow sunflowers. The strong sunshine made our cheeks grow hot and pink, although a cool wind kept us fresh. Black-and-white cows dotted some green fields. Farmers tossed hay, tried to dry it before the forecasted rain came and spoiled it. In the distance, the Jura Mountains looked blue as storm clouds built over them. A dozen sheep ran around the pasture below the playground. Their bells tinkled constantly. The young ones didn't have their tails docked yet, and they looked funny with long tails, like dogs. A lamb said 'mami', like a child calling its mother. The adult sheep all answered "mééé," not "bahbah," like in nursery rhymes. It was time to go home, or we'd have sunstroke.

As Canada became a distant reality, I wondered if this was home. Even though to some we might be considered "outsiders" or foreigners, we felt integrated in our community. My family seemed to be mostly well here now, and I supposed it didn't really matter where we lived as long as we had each other, but this was a pretty nice place to live—as an immigrant, a local or whatever. Maybe it didn't really matter after all.

Multiculturalism, affirmative philosophy, cultural assimilation and social integration? Theories. The daily reality I encountered was a blend of a bit of everything: cultural mosaic, melting pot, acceptance, racism, social inequality, equal opportunity, traditions, distortion of national identity, rich culture, ethno-racial tensions, social and economic integration, acceptance, refusal . . . Life as a migrant is lived by each differently. My experience, for the most part, has been positive and enriching, but I see migrants and refugees who struggle every day. I understand my journey was perhaps unusual, even easy, and I am thankful. Migrant assimilation is assessed by four primary factors: socioeconomic status, geographic distribution, second-language attainment and intermarriage. My journey, social scientists would likely say, was favoured by my circumstances.

When I came back to Switzerland, I felt privileged to belong to two nations, two cultures. To be home in both. To completely blend in both. That might not have been realistic.

My mother is British, and I now realize that I can never really be considered fully Swiss. My ways are influenced by my British mother, my Swiss childhood, my Canadian life. I will never be as Swiss as my cousin in the village who lives next door to his parents, who has never left, who knows nothing but what it is to be Swiss. But, really, I don't want to be like that. I'm quite happy to have a more diverse background and view of humanity, even if it means that in some small way I might be an outsider in every country. A foreigner. Migration, this time around, was a choice for us: a conscious decision to change the way our life is lived. It is a choice I am happy to have made, even if now I belong nowhere and everywhere.

Oma Eguara

Twice Bitten, Twice Sly

I have migrated twice—once as a child and then again as an adult. When it happened in my childhood, I did not know that my family was migrating. I just woke up in the morning on a different continent, and that was that. When I migrated as an adult, I was aware and in control. I can say that I much preferred the second experience.

This is how it all took place. In the 1960s, many Nigerian couples travelled to England to work and study to better their lives. My parents were one such couple. Dad arrived in England first, while Mum remained in Nigeria, raising her young son and daughter. Dad soon settled in South East London, and Mum joined him the following year. My brother and sister were left in the care of our maternal grandmother and extended family.

My parents eventually bought a three-storey house in London, which was a haven to us for many years. Not too long after settling in, Mum became pregnant with me. It was the practice among the studying immigrant Nigerian community at that time to arrange private fostering for their children, so they could continue to work and study. After a few fostering attempts that did not work out too well, I was taken at eight weeks old to live with a wonderful white English family in Hampshire, the Knights.*

The next year, my sister Ellen* was born, and five years later my brother Jules.* They each came to live with the Knights and me. Mummy and Daddy Knight loved us as their own, and so did their three sons. We loved them, too, and though we exchanged visits with our biological parents and knew we had siblings and an extended family in Nigeria, we regarded the Knights as our family. They were our mum, dad and brothers. I did not understand then why children sneered in derision when I told them the Knight boys were my brothers. I only unravelled the puzzle years later as an adult. As a child, I was heart-blind to colour difference—I could see it with my eyes but did not feel it in my heart. It was like having socks of different colours; they were all socks, just different colours!

Sometime in the early '70s, my paternal grandfather died. Dad travelled back to Nigeria for the funeral. While there, he decided that he would not be returning to England. My mother, who was still studying and working, had a short time to wrap up her studies, pack up the house, somehow retrieve three children from a foster family they would not willingly leave and return with them to Nigeria.

I mentioned that we would not have willingly left the Knights. Imagine that they were the family we lived with from day to day, the ones who saw us take our first steps, say our first words and survive our first days at school, the ones who taught us how to stand up for ourselves against 1970s racist schoolyard taunts. They were the ones who came in the night when we cried, fussed over us when we were ill, attended parents' evenings, doctors' appointments and Brownies performances, and did all the things that parents and families do for their children. They were paid by my parents to foster us, but, without a doubt, they went above and beyond the call of duty.

Some time before my mother's relocation dilemma, when Dad still lived in England and before Jules was born, my parents invited Ellen and me to spend time with them in London. We were used to going over to London but accompanied by the Knights. We often spent weekends and school holidays there as one big black-and-white family. My parents' house was large, and there were lots of rooms to run around and get lost in. However, this time, my parents asked to have just us. There was nothing strange about this, as they were our parents. I refused, not having been anywhere without Mummy Knight since I was a baby. But happy-go-lucky Ellen went by herself. When she returned, Ellen had tales of fun, sweets, more fun and more sweets. It sounded like something I would be willing to try if the opportunity ever arose again.

Around this time, there were stories in the news about white foster families "claiming" their black foster children in the law courts. So, when it came time for my mother to return with us to Nigeria, a country we had never been to, she feared that we might refuse and make a fuss and that the Knights might apply to the courts to keep us. Consequently, she did not tell the Knights that she was relocating the family to Nigeria. And she did not tell us. My mother merely asked that we spend the summer holiday with her in London, as, without Dad, she was feeling lonely. Remembering my sister's exciting experience, and seeing that she did eventually return safely, I surprised everyone by accepting. Ellen was up for it, and Jules was bundled along.

We had a lovely summer in London with Mum, maintaining phone contact with the Knights. As the summer drew to a close, I looked forward to returning to school in September. I would be transitioning from infants' phase to juniors'. My class had been to visit our lovely, modern classroom in the brand-new building. I was excited to be one of the first children to use it.

Our usual journey from London back to Hampshire consisted of a train ride. Strangely, this time we had to have painful shots that made us feel ill and then return by plane. This was to be my, Ellen's, and Jules's first time in an airport and our first time on a plane. I can still remember the extra effort my mother made to dress us up in new clothes. She even put hairpieces and new earrings on Ellen and me.

"Ooh!" I exclaimed, looking around the busy airport. "It's so strange to be going back by plane this time."

I did not notice how nervous my mother felt at this comment. Running through a busy airport at night, trying to board the plane on time, was very different to our usual routine. Much different to walking casually on to a train platform, then stepping leisurely on to a train.

Ellen and Jules sat with Mum on one side of the aisle. I sat with a female passenger on the other.

"Why are we going back by plane, Mum?" I asked.

"Because it's faster," was her reply.

The plane ride turned out to be much longer than our train journeys. I busied myself reading storybooks and drawing pictures. I hardly slept at all. The plane eventually landed, and we alighted into searing heat. I noticed that there were a lot more black people than usual, there were palm trees everywhere and there were lizards basking in the sun.

"This is a very strange part of England," I remarked. "There are lots of black people. And lizards. And palm trees."

"You are not in England anymore," my mother replied, almost triumphantly. "You are now in Nigeria!"

After taking in the novelty, I began to remind my mother that it was Monday, the first day of school. We needed to head back quickly, or Ellen and I would be late. She managed to avoid responding to my reminders, and I got distracted by the new sights, sounds and experiences.

This is how my siblings and I were tricked into leaving England. I call it "the Great Kidnapping," our unwitting childhood migration. We had no prior knowledge and no say in the matter. We were simply ripped away from everything we knew and loved and transplanted somewhere else.

Needless to say, the Knights were devastated by the sudden loss of three children. It was like a triple bereavement, all at once. They knew and accepted that one day, in the future, we would all be leaving. But by the time they found out about it, our departure was in the past. Now, as far as they knew, they would never see or hear from us again.

Ellen and I felt tricked and betrayed, and little Jules fell ill. The doctor said he was pining for the Knights and recommended sending him back. Our parents, however, had no such plans. I soon accepted my new circumstances, as I was helpless to reverse them. Ellen, on the other hand, began to save every penny to buy a ticket back to England. In time, we acclimatized, Jules recovered and we settled into our new life in Nigeria.

We never forgot the Knights, our friends, our town and our beloved school. All the Knight boys had attended this school, and so had Mummy Knight. I had looked forward to graduating from it and moving on to a local college, a dream that was never to be.

My father began posting letters from us to the Knights. It was wonderful to receive their replies. Over the years, Ellen and I kept our resolve that as soon as we were old enough, we would return to England. Jules, however, has no memory of our life before the Great Kidnapping.

We shared our growing-up years with the Knights in our letters —common entrance exams, secondary school, boarding house, A Levels, university, boyfriends and eventually marriage and motherhood. Ellen and I looked forward to getting jobs and paying our own way back to England. Our parents would have no part in it. They feared that we would marry English boys and they would never see us again.

Fast-forward thirty-two years from the Great Kidnapping.

I had four children and an unhappy marriage, with emotional abuse in the mix. My husband now lived in London, England, while I and the children lived in Lagos, Nigeria.

By this time, Ellen had fought relentlessly to obtain a British passport in Nigeria. It was not an easy feat, as the onus was on her to prove her British citizenship to the embassy staff. I had begun the process before her. However, a long list of near-impossible-to-obtain evidence was required. Being newly pregnant and having recently lost my ten-week-old son, I decided to put the process on hold until after the baby. Ellen, newly married at the time, managed to scrape together the required evidence, endure the patronising treatment of the embassy staff, obtain her British passport and relocate to England. The Knights were overjoyed. They had given up hope of ever seeing any of us again.

With the unhappy state of my marriage, the emotional abuse, societal stigma towards single mothers in Nigeria and the difficulties of single parenting, I decided to return to the UK. I did my research and found that my children could have a much better life in England than they presently had in Nigeria. I would migrate again, this time with full preparation. There would be no hasty night flights and no secret plans. My extended family and children were fully in support.

Once again, I resumed the battle to prove my British citizenship. My mother had travelled with our names on her passport, so we had no travel documents of our own. With the groundwork laid down by Ellen, I had a more solid case. The law gave my four children British citizenship by descent. It took nearly two years to process our passports. Finally, thirty-five years after the Great Kidnapping, I would be returning to England!

I was under no illusion that life in England would be easy. My teaching degree from a Nigerian university and years of teaching experience did not qualify me to teach in UK schools. I had to return to school and retrain as a teacher. I eventually completed a master's degree and have begun a doctorate program.

It did not take long for my children to settle in. They started school and filled their days with schoolwork. They made friends and picked up London accents. The older ones took part-time jobs and began to enjoy the taste of economic independence. Two, as I write, are now graduates of British universities and steadily climbing the career ladder. The other two are not far behind. My eldest has given me two grandchildren; I now have a little interracial clan!

The day I took my children to visit the Knights was the day a dream of nearly forty years came true. Daddy Knight had passed away, and Mummy Knight was now a silver-haired great-grandmother. The family had expanded from three boys to include several grandchildren and great-grandchildren and their spouses and partners. At last, Mummy Knight's long-lost African daughters had returned. In all the years since the Great Kidnapping, she had sent me, Ellen and Jules birthday and Christmas cards with a little spending money tucked inside. She still sends them to this day and now also to our children.

I look back and am thankful that I made the choice to migrate. There have been very many difficult times, but it has all been worth it. The lessons I have learned from my two migrations have left me twice bitten and twice sly. I now have the uncanny habit of saving every bit of paperwork, including shopping and cash-machine receipts, in case we have to prove something. I take photographs documenting every stage and phase of our lives, in case we ever have to prove who we are again. And I have every report card and certificate for each of my children. You never can tell if they will need it someday for a migration journey of their own.

After all of this, my recommendations for all would-be immigrants are thus:

1. Keep all informed.

Explain your plans to your children, whether you plan to leave them behind or take them along. Adapting to a new country, climate and culture is never an easy task. Having Mummy or Daddy migrate without an explanation could be even more traumatising. In our case, the trauma was experienced by several people—five members of the Knight family, the family and friends who supported them, plus Ellen, Jules and me.

2. Research your new country and prepare.

Learn as much as you can before the big move—lifestyle and societal norms; requirements for work, education, entrepreneurship or whatever you plan to do when you get there; healthcare; housing; local communities of your countrymen and women for support. Find out what documentation you will need, and take it along with you. It can take longer and become complicated if you try to obtain it from your new location. Fortunately, I had my educational certificates and school transcripts, plus my children's school reports and immunization records. It helped us all to settle in quickly.

3. Integrate.

The sooner you integrate into your new country, the sooner you will recover from the upheaval of migration and begin to move on. Learn the language; sample the food; socialise; learn about the political terrain and how this affects you; begin to build a support network; volunteer to gain work experience, references and a taste of the new working world. The human interaction can also keep you from feeling lonely and insignificant.

4. Maintain ties.

This may not make sense to everyone who migrates. Some may be escaping adverse situations which require severing ties. However, if it is safe and makes sense for you, stay in touch with the family, friends and culture you left behind. This can help to retain your identity and provide grounding when all around is new and changing.

5. Get help.

Find out what help exists to facilitate your immigration and integration. You may benefit from joining a support group for immigrant women. Before I left for England, I researched online and via telephone calls. I looked into childcare, employment and education. I was able to take advantage of free enterprise and skills trainings, grants for enterprise and community projects, schemes to support women and ethnic minorities, support to recover from emotional abuse and, eventually, student loans for my children and me. I got help with housing and legal aid. Knowing that I was not alone and that assistance was available helped me to re-establish myself where I had no other support system. This may also help with your choice of new location, as some places are more supportive than others.

Migration can be a very daunting project which can take years to plan and execute. Perhaps even more so if managed alone or as a single parent with children. Even with an overall plan, I learned to take one day at a time. I learned to manage setbacks, delays and disappointments with optimism, while keeping my eyes on the end goal. Migration may not be easy, but it can work with careful planning and support. Many women have succeeded and are now happy in their new homelands. To those contemplating migration, I say: You deserve a happy and fulfilled life. You have the power to achieve it. If migration will make this happen for you, go, sister, go for it!

Names have been changed.